THE FLOWERING ROCK

THE FLOWERING ROCK

COLLECTED POEMS 1938-1974

E.M. ROACH

COMPILED BY DANIELLE GIANETTI
EDITED BY KENNETH RAMCHAND

INTRODUCTION

KENNETH RAMCHAND

PEEPAL TREE

First published in Great Britain in 1992
New and Revised Edition 2012
Peepal Tree Press
17 King's Avenue
Leeds LS6 1QS
Yorkshire
England

ISBN 13: 9781845232078

Supported using public funding by
ARTS COUNCIL
ENGLAND

CONTENTS

Unpublished Poems

Appendix of alternative versions

FOREWORD

This is an extremely important book. Before its appearance no literary historian or critic, let alone lover of poetry, will have been able to measure the full richness of West Indian poetic creation in the era since the Second World War. One always suspected that Eric Roach was one of the major West Indian poets. This book consolidates his name in a pantheon which includes at least Claude McKay, Derek Walcott, Louise Bennett, Martin Carter, and Edward Kamau Brathwaite.

The *Collected Poems* rescues E.M. Roach from the anthologies. When one knows a poet only from old magazines, anthologies feeding on previous anthologies, and mention of his work in a few critical essays and occasional erudite articles, the impact is bound to be provisional, piecemeal, disintegrated, desultory and profoundly unsatisfactory. The work glimmers, scintillates at its best, catches the eye, gleams in the memory but cannot *shine* outright. The presence of the poet in the imagination is not whole until his work is brought together full-bodied and complete in spirit in some definitive collection such as this.

This is not the time or the place to attempt a full critical study of Roach's *Collected Poems.* But this work now waits to be done and one hopes it is done soon. And to accompany a full scale study we need a memoir of the poet's life and times to set the work in context. Enough for now, however, marvellously enough, are the poems of this remarkable poet and powerful West Indian literary pioneer together in one book to remind us, if we need reminding, of the richness of our heritage to which this book adds so much.

That heritage, in its poetic form, Roach helped to mould at a crucial time. He was one of the first to express in remarkable poetry and clear individual voice the vision of a precise and distinctive West Indian identity. In unforced, vivid detail he writes his descriptions of landscape and people and suggests insights into nature, history and personality which are specifically West Indian in their inspiration and, because so true, wholly universal in their impact. We tend to forget how unusual a really authentic West Indian voice was in those early days of overwhelmingly derivative verse – derivative verse, what is more, derived more often than not from the most Romantic and lachrymose English tradition. Roach went far beyond all that.

In fact, what Roach derived from the English poetic tradition was strength, not jingling flabbiness. I find exceptional how successfully he assimilates English literary, and also Biblical, influences in his poetry. He does not copy, he absorbs and makes what he has absorbed part of a new way of declaring his own love and vision in his own land among his own, most often grimly poor, people.

I think what I respond to most is Roach's passion for the land and the people, both of which are so clearly and categorically West Indian. The intense feeling that informs his best poetry – and so much of the poetry is good, which is another thing this book brings out – expresses a very specific yearning for a shared identity which will leap over island isolation and bind together our fragmented historical consciousness into a coherent whole. We read him and we think again how much more important poets are to politicians in our regional context.

Since I was a student I have known and loved a number of Eric Roach's poems. "To My Mother", "March Trades", "Homestead", "I am the Archipelago" were among the first poems to light my imagination. "Seven splendid cedars break the trades…" breathes a music that will be with me as long as I live. His great poems were inescapably part of my nurturing and the nurturing of countless other West Indians. However, I never knew he had written so many poems and so many of them so beautiful. We are all in the debt of the indefatigable finder and collector of these poems, Danielle Gianetti, her mentor and encourager, Ken Ramchand, and the publisher, Jeremy Poynting, with his pioneering, wonderfully productive, infinitely valuable Peepal Tree Press. Through all these, Eric Roach, in his *Collected Poems,* lives a new life and that life of enduring poetic creation is magnified a hundredfold.

Ian McDonald
1992

PUBLISHER'S NOTE ON THE TEXT

This second edition of E.M. Roach's collected poems takes the opportunity to correct some mis-transcriptions, some printer's errors and to add some significant variants of key poems. Since the 1992 publication of *Flowering Rock*, in 2008 we published Laurence A. Breiner's monograph, *Black Yeats: Eric Roach and the Politics of Caribbean Poetry*, and it is to Larry Breiner's research and very helpful notes on errors, and suggestions for essential variants that the improvements to this edition are indebted. His fuller bibliographical listing of published poems has been used to replace that in the first edition.

We planned to add three early poems published in the *Trinidad Guardian*, "To Learie", "Dancer" and "June Blazes", but unfortunately only the first of these could be transcribed with any level of confidence. We have added variants of "Anacaona" (*Trinidad Guardian*, 1949), the 1951 *Bim* text of "The Old House", two versions of "Homestead" (from *Kyk-over-Al*, 1957, and from *The Sun's Eye*, 1968 – the existing version came from *Caribbean Quarterly* in 1952); the significant variant of "Poem (Pray that the Poem Come out of the Dark)" (*Kyk-over-Al*, 1957); the version of "A Reed for my Rime" broadcast on the *Caribbean Voices* programme in 1954, and an earlier version of "City Centre '70". As *Black Yeats* shows, Eric Roach was a constant reviser of his poems, in particular moving in a trajectory from the particular to the more general. The addition of these variants allows readers to trace that process and make their own judgements. At some point we plan a more extensive edition with variant readings and notes, but this edition is not it.

This edition corrects the following errors:

"A Lover Speaks" (p. 49). The penultimate line has been corrected. "Then shall my fancy be not free". The first edition had "Then shall my fancy not be free".

"She" (p. 54). Line 6 has been corrected: "From old continents, and the commingling…". The first edition had "Of old continents…"

"March Trades" (p. 58). The last line of stanza one has been corrected: "Sturdier than savagery of wind and sea". The first edition had "sun and sea".

"Shallow Underground" (pp. 60-61). The first edition mangled the sequencing of this poem (it was the days of phototypesetting and manual imposition) by printing the last seven stanzas of the poem on the page before the title and only the first three stanzas under the title. This has been corrected.

"The Old Man" (p. 63) The last line of the fifth stanza has been corrected: "Upon an opening ocean". The first edition had "Upon the opening ocean".

"Homestead" (pp. 85-86). We have corrected "paisan" to "paysan".

"Letter to Lamming" (pp. 87-88). The first edition omitted line 6 of the last stanza: "Young men's tin percussion".

"Haitian Trilogy" (pp. 96-99). In "Black Kings", the second line of the fourth stanza, "Up-hurled his passionate spirit" has been corrected from "He hurled his passionate spirit".

In "A Tear for Toussaint" (pp. 98-99), the last twelve lines printed in the first edition have been deleted, since they belong to the following script (by Harold Telemaque) in the BBC *Caribbean Voices* files.

"I Walk Abroad" (pp. 102-103). The fourth line of stanza three has been corrected to "I take Caribbean nature". The first edition had "I take my Caribbean nature".

"To My Mother" (p. 130) The later version printed in *Caribbean Poetry Now* has a small variation in stanzas 4 and 5 which is worth noting: "[…] you crawl up/ Your broken stairs like Golgatha, and all the dead/ Beckon your dying bones… // I do not mourn, but all my love/ Praise life's continuity the endless year/ […]".

Jeremy Poynting
2012

INTRODUCTION

KENNETH RAMCHAND

On the morning of April 17, 1974, Eric Merton Roach travelled to Siparia, "south town of quiet ways". From there, he penetrated further south, "beyond Mendez", to arrive at last at "land's end in Quinam Bay". The road he took is described in one of his last poems as "a black canal to the sea".

Now at the famous bay, Eric Roach drank the insecticide he had been careful to provide himself with; from the spot where he imagined Columbus had landed, he swam out into the green sea. It was a literary death, the *finis* inscribed at the end of a stubbornly literary life. Among the unpublished scripts Roach left neatly labelled on his desk, was the poem "At Quinam Bay", written a few months earlier and entered in a literary competition organised to mark the 25th Anniversary of the University of the West Indies. In this poem, the poet returns, as he does again and again throughout his writing career, to the figure of Columbus, seeing him now as "weary of the sea", "sick in flesh" and "sick at heart". The poem traces this malaise down the centuries, in slaver as well as in slave, a pageant of guilt and futility suffered vicariously by the all-seeing figure who emerges at the end of the poem:

> bone-weary as Colon himself,
> soul-wretched as the slavers' crews
> heartsick as any dying slave
> he walks to bay
> every dream he dreamed long drowned,
> every love sunk underground...

Like the figure in the poem, Roach was in despair. He had come to feel that his life had produced nothing but "shards and shingles of loose words" and that his poems were being swept like "black leaves in drought/ Into the limbo of this evil century". But this was not the simple and egoistic despair of a man thinking that success in the world had passed him by. Roach was committed, as selflessly and as passionately as one can be, to the idea of a unique Caribbean civilisation taking shape out of the implosion of cultures and peoples in the region. The ultimate justification of his art would be that it contributed to the making and understanding of this new, cross-cultural civilisation.

But Roach never flattered himself that such commitments alone could automatically make poetry or the poet. You might hold the most revolutionary views with the greatest sincerity, and still count for nothing as a poet. And like Yeats, the poet he most admired, Roach felt that "Too long a sacrifice/ Can make a stone of the heart". As late as 1971 (too late perhaps), he was reminding young, angry voices that "we must write out of the totality of our history, our environment and our feeling".

Writing that comes out of such a totality helps us to recognise the contradictions in our nature as human animals, and may ideally help us to achieve some sort of order and balance, if only for a moment. Such writing can never be guilty of the stridency and the possible play-acting of those with doctrinaire and partisan solutions to social problems.

But in order to write out of such a totality one needs all the artifice of fiction, one has to employ all the expressive capacity that comes from the most religious attention to craft. For Roach, a poet, especially as a young poet, is a reader of other poets, and a strict practitioner of craft, an experimenter and an innovator yes, but a believer, always seeking after the appropriate form. So, in Roach's work, the resounding iambic lines of the early poems, the dutiful use of rhyme and formal stanza give way under the pressure of tiring faith and stretched feelings to more open and jagged forms, and finally, in the poems after 1970, to an invisibly regulated free verse (which is what all good free verse is).

In the early poems (1938-1949), published in obscure places

mostly under the name "Merton Maloney", Roach turned self-consciously, and with mild contention, to his own landscape ("A mountain top with cap of silver snow/ I have not seen"), taking delight in naming its bright plumed birds, its forest trees, its lively landscapes and its flaming immortelles ("Immortelles", 1938). But his delight in the landscape as and for itself did not argue against seeing the landscape as vessel and medium containing truths about people and place. It was the poet's dangerous duty to come up "through a chasm of earth", come "up from that darkness" and interpret those truths "with the earth's rich rhythms" ("Colour, for Harold Telemaque", 1947).

One of the things he came up with and held on to, long before the folk had become part of the politics of our intellectual life, was the nature of the peasant's relationship to the land. He writes about this in one of his most famous and resonant poems, "Homestead", first published in 1952, but revised repeatedly up to 1968. In this poem he celebrates a father figure, a peasant, a slave man's son:

> The man is dead but I recall
> Him in my voluntary song.
> His life was unadorned as bread,
> He reckoned weathers in his head
> And wore their ages on his face
> And felt their keenness to his bone
> The sting of sun and whip of rain,
> And saw the quality of morning
> In the sunset mask of evening

But Roach was not one of our middle-class microphone pastoralists, he was not one to escape into what he knew was being destroyed and lost. It should be noticed too, that even while he was ostensibly singing about the present struggle of the free man, there is a backward glance ("The sting of sun and whip of rain") at the achievement of those who had slaved before. In "Poets and Paint-ers", he calls upon painters, poets, thinkers and strugglers not so much to emulate the peasant as to carry on with the work:

My father the strong man
Could set his stamp upon
The sterile fields of clay or stone;
With mattock, hoe and spade, the good couth tools
He wrote his will upon such stubborn earth
And charmed sweet harvests forth.
And are we lesser pioneers than he?

It is not misleading to say that the early Roach was a positive poet who found symbols of strength and beauty in people ("To My Mother"), in the landscape, in man-made things, and in nature. The great hawk in "Frigate Bird Passing" (1950), is very much a hawk, but he is also poetic energy soaring, as in the poem, "Beyond" (1950). Yet even at this early stage, the poet is conscious of the inevitable passing (the word sits so innocently in the title of the poem):

He flies and dreams.
His hard sure instinct beams him on
While steep beneath him sleeps the green sea death
That shall immobilise his viking wing ...

Death and darkness lurk even in the very early poems. Among these poems two are entitled, significantly, "Death on Sunday" (1943), and "A Poet Passes" (1938); then, there is a poem on the death of the day ("Dusk", 1948) and one on the death of the year ("New Year", 1938); "Tonight, Tomorrow", (1939), sees sleep as being close to death and invokes day and light to bring the person in the poem back to "the dignity of life"; yet another of these early poems seeks to deny death a final say by celebrating the sounds that live eternally ("Sounds Live", 1948). Finally, it is darkness, the darkness of sky, tree and hill that dominates "A Night of Stars", (1938). The sombre note is struck in nearly every poem.

In the early period of his life and work, however, Roach has enough hope and optimism to beat back his darkest anxieties. The poet possessed and was possessed by his Caribbean landscape – by sea and rock and sky – and you can hear and feel an elation in poems like "I Walk Abroad" (1953), that might almost serve to suppress intimations of the great dark, and to banish any thought of alienation or loss:

> This is my own.
> I join my voice to the frog-throat in the pond,
> To cricket shrill and bird-cry in the wood;
> I sign my name upon the papyrus
> Of plantain leaves broad in my garden,
> I'm halo'd with the sun.

Roach knew and felt early that if you belonged to the land, and it belonged to you, then everything else would be added in its proper place. It is for this reason that he can claim his Africanity with the same fervour that Claude McKay and Aimé Césaire claimed theirs. His Africanity was only a part, though a fundamental part, of his Caribbean nature and identity:

> This is I.
> Under my dazzling skies in my day's fullness,
> Under my African transplanted skin
> I take my Caribbean nature,
> Under my continental negroid hair the skull
> Assumes the infinite variety, shapes and moods of
>   islands

But as the rhetoric and insistence in the poems indicate, Roach had to keep whipping himself into line. One of the struggles in the early poems is that with his own temperament, his own sinking sense of the individual's relation to Time and the Universe. Troubled by intimations of mortality and transience, he sought comfort in the human striving to achieve, reading it as the way to overcome time, and to snatch permanence out of flux. This is how he understood the peasant's relationship to the land, and the relationship of poets and painters to their art. Homer and Milton, he declares in "The Blind Weavers", "are taller than time", and their "proud poems/ March with immortal/ And majestic tread/ Through each applauding generation".

But Roach was no blind weaver. He was very alive to the social, political and cultural issues in his time and place, and these were just as real to him as, and not separate from, his more philosophical concerns. As we have seen, he never had a problem with Africa: he was proud of his Africanity but did not think of himself as an African or as someone removed from his natural habitat. In his "Haitian Trilogy" (1953), he traces the passage to the Caribbean of the Dahomean serpent god, Damballa, attributing to him an inspiring role in the Haitian revolution. The poet goes on in this poem to reflect on the outcome of that much-sabotaged revolution, praising the Black Kings but noticing the ironies in their "mangled victory". For Toussaint himself, there is admiration, and a tear for that fighter, dungeoned in winter, forbidden hope's sun. The poem ends with the prayer that islands may still hope with Toussaint's heart, "And climbers try his cliff path up the hill/ Between the white outrage and the black forbearance".

Roach makes dramatic use of dialect in the opening section of this poem to suggest the bewilderment of the enslaved people and their anxious supplication to gods and ancestors. In "Ballad of Canga" it is dialect that he uses to give communal body to the narrating voice, and to portray an anancy quality in the old Ashantee man. In most of the poems, however, Roach does what our better poets are generally content to do, and that is, to maintain the dialect tone: the West Indian accent would carry the stress and intonation of the dialect, and would gear into dialect itself when required by the inner dynamics of the poem. His use of folk material was just as instinctive, authentic, and unostentatious.

His treatment of history, including slavery and the aftermath is just as purist and exemplary. For Roach, the blood of Carib and Arawak are proclaimed in the hibiscus, and traces of all that happened here in history, not only since Columbus but long before that rude intervention, are carried in soil and sky and sea. And so, his singing of the landscape is itself an embrace of the peoples of the Caribbean and their history.

But he also makes direct and powerful reference to specific historical episodes. In the English-speaking Caribbean, is there anyone who had written as passionately about slavery and its devastations before "I am the Archipelago" (1957), hit our colonised eardrums?

> My language, history and my names are dead
> And buried with my tribal soul. And now
> I drown in the groundswell of poverty
> No love will quell. I am the shanty town,
> Banana, sugar-cane and cotton man
> Economies are soldered with my sweat...

In "Something Seen" (1952), the poet recognises the continuing terms of enslavement in the "ill-paid large-tasked labour" of present times, and, after warning that "A bitter fruit will ripen on our tree", he argues that instead of freedom and possibility there has come or continued a "deliberate cleavage of the island climate".

Well into the 1950s, Roach invested in the hope of there being created in the islands, out of the sufferings of the past and out of the meeting of cultures, a civilisation blessed "With equal freedoms and with common love", a civilisation that would have learnt "To take the buffet/And to prosper in it."

In "Invocation", a poem of 1949, he calls upon the sun to make dry the swamps and marshes of the soul, and he beseeches the stars of his fate to draw out the poisonous hate that rises when he counts "the burning whip weals one by one". As long as he could believe in such possibility, he could hold off the darkness. He could devote his energies as a poet to creating songs and images of light against the impending gloom.

But it was never easy for this buffeted creature. "Oh no more now/ Ascends the heart/ Like the green bough" he declares in a poem of 1949, only to bounce back in 1950 with "The Flowering Rock" declaring that "Our hearts break not/ Though they are forever broken". But the more insistent the assertions of faith and hope in these poems, the more we suspect the dark pressures of unbelief beating upon the heart. Already, in 1950, in the poem entitled "Beyond", he is urging the poet to direct his song into "the glorious landscapes of the soul"; and in "Death Does Not" he denies that death can "Silence our singing love./ If but the record's made/ Some ear will hear it played". This is true, but it is a desperate thing for a living creature to have to be clinging to in the middle of a life.

Unlike his frigate bird passing, Roach could not power his way through as if "the green sea death" did not exist. In a brief article entitled "Blues for Eric Roach", Gordon Rohlehr suggests that the poet's mind was filled with images of death since 1961. It is true that the phenomenon became more pronounced with the publication of "He Juggles Images" in 1961, in which one of the images is of the poet "… drowned and sucked under the sea/ Down to the never never tide", but with all the poems available at last, we can see that death was on Roach's mind from the early 1940s, and that there is more than an element of bravado in the poet's adoption of the hawk and the rock as his coat of arms.

By 1960 in truth, Roach had given up hope in the coming of the political kingdom. On the positive side he had written the inspirational "Homestead", the self-creating "To My Mother", and the wilful "Despite Ancestral Rape". He had warned his fellow poet Cecil Herbert that "To be silent in our silent air/ Is suicide". He had written an ambitious poem about origins, about love, about the muse, about the landscape, about history and the healing process, and about the high destiny of the humble poet, and called it "Lady by the Sea". He had also written the more directly nationalistic "The Fighters" in which he opens "the dead well of history of our wretched race", to claim as his own the strength of those Black men in the public eye who had grown tall through fighting; and he finds, what Lamming was to pick up for discussion later, that "Deep down in the deep seam, the water's clear/ And clean from the black rock of Africa."

But the West Indian Federation had come and gone, dashing his hopes for harmony between islands. He had seen but did not join the exodus of literary talent in the 1960s. He felt the emptiness of the Independence each island crept into out of the demise of the Federation. He saw the new waves of cultural imperialism making for the islands. Even before all this, he had written "Truth in my calypso is out of tune/ I am to hum a foreign cansonet", ("In Mango Shade", 1953); he had also written "A Dirge for a Dead Poet" (1954), in which he comments wryly: "But not my unfulfilled/ Living I mourn here/ In these dry cadences,/ My unended dying". Could he still "recreate the world on islands"?

Judging from the poems of the 1960s and 1970s, the answer was a more and more emphatic "No". "The Old Woman" (1960) sitting alone in her cottage making friends with the dust is a figurative prelude to this phase of Roach's work. The reverend attitude of "Lady by the Sea" is succeeded by the tone of bewilderment in one who has served the muse, his love, and the islands but has had no comfort except to rail at "The Curse of Her Beauty".

A measure of the deepening despair felt by the poet can be gained by comparing the positives in the earlier "The Fighters" and "For A. A. Cipriani" (1959), with three poems of the 1970s – "Blues for Uncle Tom' (1972), 'Elegy for N. Manley' (1972), and 'Ballad For Tubal Butler" (1972). Captain Cipriani is celebrated as poet of humanity, "indestructible as legend", but for Roach, Martin Luther King has been degraded by an age of hate "whose actors sweat their barren seeds of blood/that know no resurrection, lord,/no easter morning for our mourning." The Manley poem emphasises his decrepitude, and the waste that was all his hope, work and faith; and the erstwhile proud and raging Butler has become "a poor buffoon", and "a toothless hound whining at his private fleas". Roach is compassionate towards these heroes who were made futile by time, by those benefiting from the status quo, and by a public ultimately unresponsive to care.

But he is scathing towards the more recent politicians "the grappe of fools" who have taken power in the land. The people of the islands wanted a federation, "But asses brayed/ And the brittle dream shattered/ To shards of cays and shoals/ That pricked our hearts to tears". In "The Pharaoh's Eye" (unpublished), Roach follows the rise and the decline of a politician who raised expectations to a high pitch and then withdrew till "seeing his act,/ our stunned hands stopped applauding".

The continuance of racial division in the islands, ("these rank simian hatreds/ of customs, skins and creeds") meant that the dream of a vital creole culture would be denied beyond the poet's time to wait. There was further disappointment in the growth of emigration, ("… the best bolt off/ into the endless masquerade of exile") and in the steady drift from the countryside to "the stink of slums/ the lethal rage and grief of ghettos". It is this strong antipathy to the vagrant and loveless life of our cities that makes the reminiscing of "Verse in August" more of a lament for a mode of being needlessly lost than an exercise in maudlin autobiography or nostalgia.

To Roach in the 1970s, we had become "mini-men on rocks", perverted souls rushing headlong like the Gadarene swine, or poised to leap like the doomed Caribs "over the precipice to the shrouding sea". Our condition is described thus in the unpublished poem "Senghor Visiting": "This flock of rocks, fleece/ of the grand Columban legend/ shorn now of innocence, butchered/ by churches wars and politics". His final and most comprehensive image for a condition that the poem wants us to feel as being also a universal condition is declared in the title of the poem "Littering Earth's Centre". In this poem Roach goes over the history of the diaspora, looking at how we missed becoming what we might have been, and worrying once more about the significance of the artist's arrival on the scene, a worry that is also a question about the meaning of his own life:

> Ask Brathwaite who sent him.
> Ask him to write that poem of himself
> Streaming through the loins of slave on slave
> century on century
> to this outpouring of his crafted verse
> Ask Walcott too,
> he talks like a wise man
> disdainful, cool, offhand, ironical.
> And ask that cold sardonic man
> Making the perfect fiction,
> Wrinkling his Brahman nose at islands

Unlike later West Indian writers, Roach was steeped in the work of his contemporaries. He was also steeped in Western literature. But there were no answers for his beleaguered soul in his dialogue with the great living or dead. He had found it difficult to see the disturbances of 1970 as anything more than an uncharted and incompetent expression of a profound social malaise. He was disappointed in his hopes for his society, the world, and himself but he would not follow spurious gods. Not surprisingly, he got into wars in the 1970s with armchair radicals, aestheticians of the grassroots, neo-Africanists and people who either had not read his work or who could not afford to expose themselves to contradiction and uncertainty. Absurdly, he was accused of being against Africa, against the folk and against the dialect. He was an Afro-Saxon, he was obsolete. But the sinking poet was still moving on, beyond the narrow limits of the so-called radicals with their manly rhetoric.

As late as 1973, he was looking to measure the self-mutilations of our world and the larger male-oriented world, wondering who held us together, who "would not yield/to night nor nothing" and who might have saved us from being ashamed "to fight/those last and hardest battles with ourselves". For a man of his age and his generation this was a hard poem to write, one that bruised even the unthinkingly chauvinist mind, but with "I Say it was the Women", Roach was pointing to the most humane justification for the feminist cause. He had made the case in previous poems for the muse, the goddess and a landscape summed up as "She"; now, at the end, he found them all in the dark earnest faces of teacher, sister, mother, and wife, all the living women he knew in his time. "I die maintaining this/It was the women who restored us", he declared.

> and in my last dry season going blind,
> I look on you who would not yield
> to night nor nothing
> I know the end's not chaos,
> that you have shaped an end, a destiny
> and we shall grow
> though we ourselves
> would silence you...

It was a possible new beginning, but Roach was by now a tired man. He had lifted up sound and images of light to beat back the impending gloom, but the darkness overwhelmed him at last, "the fireflies died/ life's candles flickered out", and sound became silence as a man "passed into the heart of darkness."

Trinidad 1992.

PUBLISHED POEMS 1938-1973

NEW YEAR

In a wealth of sunny days
  The Old Year's gone;
And in this midnight
  With a people's praise
The New Year comes shining on.

I know what you shall give us
  Unknown New Year:
Laughter and high joy
  You'll smile upon us
And between a staining tear.

I know too that you bring us
  Weariness and pain,
Peace and calm content
  You'll sure not give us;
Our desiring these is vain.

Yet young Year, we welcome you,
  Go gently with us;
Friendlily and slow;
  You hoist our hopes anew,
O year, be kindly with us.

1938: as Merton Maloney

A NIGHT OF STARS

It is a night of Stars,
At dusk I saw them starting out
Into the dullened depths of sky;
Now they are set about in hosts,
And all are trembling, as though
A little wind does lull them as it passes by.

It is a night of Stars,
A still kind night that holds the hush
For sleeping. The unnumbered suns
Are strewn carelessly, lavishly
In the lap of space, and flush
Their ways with light they radiate in countless numbers.

It is a night of Stars,
A darkness swelters earth like deep
Soft sorrow on the mind of man.
The trees are high and darker heaps
Of darkness; and the hills are clad
In sober sombreness against the starlit sky.

1938: as Merton Maloney

28

IMMORTELLES

The forest flames! Look yonder in the vale.
The forest flames! Look over the green hill.
See the great immortelles like torches blaze,
And the wide woodland with their wonder fill.

The forest flames! O joy in January!
O glory on this island's woodland world!
Now that spread green is all bedecked with red,
The turning days a welcome magic hold.

The forest flames! Burst forth my song,
And bound along the pathways of the sky
Warbling high honour to the floral fire
That loosed thee from thy mute captivity!

Burst forth my song! Let tropic beauties own
A queen is now ascended to her throne.

1938: as Merton Maloney

IMMORTELLES

Earth decks herself with beauty everywhere;
A mountain top with cap of silver snow
I have not seen, but heard it lovely; here,
Bright plumèd birds are splendid things we know,
And lively landscapes rolling grandly green,
And forest trees are blazon'd o'er with bloom.
Among these giant grandees, I have seen
The imperial immortelle, with scarlet plume,
Hold courtly state, when all the forest round
Seemed palled with poverty. Come drought, come dew,
Come sun, come showers, its glory still is found
When the old year is turning round to new,
And after; through the dry and droughty days
Of first and second months its splendour stays.

1938: as Merton Maloney

DISCOVERY

I sing to the sailor Christobal Colon
The adventurous-hearted, daring discoverer.

In an age of sailing men, roving, discovering,
A ship's captain he, purposeful, bold.

The wandering spirit was vital within him
Epic adventure stirred in his soul.

In blue Mediterranean his voyaging took him.
Soon Iceland saw him, the gusts of the north.

Think of him dreaming, dreaming a day
Of visiting India, voyaging west.

The unknown ocean spread like a carpet
Monotonous hued to horizon's rim.

"The great sea of darkness".
But if a tale were true, Vikings once driven
Like straw in the storm, rode to an anchorage
On a strange land way out in the west;
What land could it be?

A tale like red wine from the presses of Spain
Quickened his heart beats, stirring his blood.

II

Behold him suffering the frowns of great kings,
Taunts of their sycophants, mockery of fools;

Till Spain thrust him out upon the Unknown,
Three cockle ships venturing, and brave men he found.

Westward they came, voyaging westward;
Into the sunset set were the helms.

III

Atlantic roared and rolled down upon them,
The Trade Winds shrieked, howled wildly at them.

Clouds and blue skies, the stars of the night,
The sun at his rising their hope of the world.

Still they held on voyaging westward,
Forever westward voyaging on.

In that strange sea of sea-borne herbage
The nadir days of dreary despair descended upon them.

The stoutest hearts quailed; the hardiest wept
And prayed to the saints for a sight of the land.

"O Holy Saviour, merciful Saviour
Have mercy upon us perishing men."

So praying and weeping, watching and waiting,
Bitterly sighing, voyaging on.

Then, "Land ahead! Land!" a masthead man shouted,
And there sure enough, like a ghost from the sea,
Like a mist of the evening, a mirage of madmen,
The gray mountain stood.
And "Oh, San Salvador!" the Admiral shouted;
Like Ulysses coming home from the sea,
Home from his wanderings, he kissed the new earth,
Kissed it and wept, and called it strange names,
Praising the saints for a feel of the land.

Thus was a world sought for and found,
Out of the Unknown sought for and found.

On a later day sailing, more southerly sailing
A third voyage making, he Iere found.

Three hills clothed in mist stood dreamlike before him,
Earth's highest emblem, the Trinity of God.

Now today from the sea his caravels come,
Come as they came four centuries gone.

Still shall they come to the end of all time
Sailing from eastward; such deeds never die.

Today Colon stands the deathless Colossus
Bestriding our world, our rising New World,
The man cannot die.

1938: as Merton Maloney

DEATH ON SUNDAY

Death is my next door neighbour in this dawn;
He came upon the old man in the night
On some most holy hour; death is right
For age had looked his coming overlong;
Age being in pain, more than old flesh could bear,
And groans were most his utterance for a year.

Death was his spikenard, his balm of peace;
The acme of his hope, his heart's dear love;
A gilded thing to which he hourly strove;
He was a Jason seeking for the fleece.
What ever powers he knew, these he implored
To cut his life ship loose where it was moored.

Now has death done him to his heart's desire;
Quenched all his pain, fulfilled his holiest hope;
Released his sickened soul, given it new scope
To seek God's health, to cleanse in Holy Fire,
And who shall sing a dirge or lay a wreath
For this most joyously departed breath?
I'll write his epitaph sans name and date,
"Here lies a man who loved his present state."

1938: as Merton Maloney

A POET PASSES

To the memory of Levi A. Darlington

Closed is a sweet-voiced fountain of our song,
The summer flow is frozen at its source;
And that clear stream which through Iere flowed
Will never murmur more this side the grave.

Hushed is the harp that made sweet melodies
Enriching life and love, exalting death.
The pleasant strains that charmed Iere's ear
Shall never more burst forth this side the grave.

Hear you Iere the deep sigh I breathe
For the departed one? The moan of woe?
Ah! he like me was poor Conception's son,
He never more to sing this side the grave.

The loud lament, the tears shall pass away,
Sorrow's short-lived and cannot keep him here;
What he has done, all that he richly gave,
Shall keep him evermore this side the grave.

1938: as Merton Maloney

35

THE TRAGEDY

The old year was a Shylock in its threat
To cut a foolish forfeit of our flesh,
But Britain sent a gallant advocate
To steer us cleanly through the evil mesh.

Foiled of his hate as the defeated Jew,
The old year goes, still muttering the threat
Which he delivers to his heir the new
Who greets us now with visage sternly set.

How shall men's madness smite the heart of man
On folly's road; how deeply shall our state
Be humbled underneath this evil ban
Is our conjecture now of future fate.

We seek with sighs Bassanio's bride of peace
To haste from Belmont to our high release.

1938: as Merton Maloney

THE STAIR OF SONG

Tread lightly on the stair, stranger,
   Lightly as you go;
Ionian Homer hammered it
   Two thousand years ago.

Many feet do pass upon it,
   Up and down they go,
Since songful Homer hammered it
   Two thousand years ago.

From many lands they come, strangers
   Where'er the wild winds blow,
Footsteps swift and slow upon it
   Up and down they go.

Many footprints fading from it
   As the round years go
Many footprints strong upon it
   In a golden glow.

Here stranger, if you seek it,
   Here is Homer's toe
Glowing though he trod the stair
   Two thousand years ago.

Here divine Dante's footsteps fared
   Six hundred years ago;
Here Wordsworth walked and thought and walked
   With gentle steps and slow.

Tread lightly on the stair, stranger,
   Lightly as you go;
Ionian Homer hammered it
   Two thousand years ago.

1939

FOLLY

Softly fur-footed folly comes
Slipping through the portal door
Of the unsuspicious heart,
Bringing its feather thought.

What is thought is almost done,
And folly's thought doth swiftly run
Into the deed and breeds a store
Of further thought-deeds more and more.

What is done in folly's thought,
In folly's footsteps through the heart,
Leaves its echo on the soul;
And evermore it off and on
Reverberates and rolls on;
Age knows what foolish youth had done
For memory's echo endings run.

1939

TONIGHT, TOMORROW

From its unknown realm
Sleep beckons me
Across uncharted areas,
And I go after some unseen helm,
Knowing naught of safe conduct
Thither, nor hope of safe abode
In that uncharted land,
Or fair return upon the backward road.
The benediction of the dawn
Will come on silver chariot wheels
Over Iere rifting her with light,
Come till my body feels
The splendid urge of day,
The dignity of life,
The lure of life's eternal forward motion
And calls the soul from slumber into strife.

1939: as Merton Roach

TO LEARIE

Of famous father a most famous son
Wherever cricket has been greatly played
Wherever men discourse of wonders done
By wisden wizards – of fine feats displayed
In the great empire game, – there in renown
Is known the name of Learie Constantine
Who won and wears now cricket's triple crown.

Here in our native sun, in the cold clime
Of Northern England are his praises loud.
Here have we seen him hit a hundred, take
A grandest catch, and give the thundering crowd
A smile as though he'd done it for our sake,
And we have seen him run and leap and swing
The ball with havoc down the taut matting.

1939

NEW LOAVES

She brings new-baked brown bread into the house
    On a wooden platter,
Sets it down upon the table
    Softly without clatter.

Now there is an old fragrance in the house
    Which everybody knows,
The Assyrian and Egyptian knew it,
    Knowing not the rose.

Homer knew and loved it when a boy,
    Sniffed it on the wind,
And the homely odour stirred him
    Being old and blind.

Shakespeare the wild, the lawless boy,
    Coming in to dine
With hunger from the fields, sniffed it,
    Said, "Ah, how fine."

She turns to me and says, "Tea is ready
    And my day's work is done."
"Thank you," I say, "and do you know
    They baked in Babylon."

1943: as Merton Maloney

SONG OF THE SLEEPERS-OUT

We are the last lees of the city's sub-communities,
We are the fearful and the forlorn with hollow hungry faces.
We are the lonely and the homeless sidewalk sleepers-out.

Who shall aid us? Who shall shelter? Not the rulers of the land,
The majesties who lift the voice and never lift the hand?
Who shall aid us, who shall succour sidewalk sleepers-out?

In the frying heat of the day the pavement steams and burns,
Under freezing dews of midnight it an iceblock turns,
And nought but this for bed and bolster have sidewalk sleepers-out.

The drowning rainfall on the city floods upon your roof,
And not a sidewalk sleeper's shelter to the torrent's proof,
And we who meet the midnight's drenching are sidewalk sleepers-out.

The wind is low and our sighs seep through the shutters of the town,
And not the shrieking hurricane can sighs of suffering drown
The sighing and the moaning of the sidewalk sleepers-out.

The lights of mercy are extinguished from the city's streets,
The lamps of charity are low and human love retreats
From the sad and shameful sojourn of the sidewalk sleepers-out.

1944

TRIBUTE TO WINIFRED ATWELL

For us the rapture and for you the roses
And the round glad waves of our applause.
You wrought us there a world within our world
Of stress and strife and traffic; an hour of charm,
An hour of delight that cannot die
Until life's day leans down and the sun sets.
For it's a golden graving on our thought
A beauty from the burin of your heart.

For this, bouquets of roses are no price;
Beauty that perishes may not requite
The imperishable hour. Grace is not dead.
What tribute too, this wreath of windy words,
This light inodorous flowering of the spirit,
This shoddy sonnet writ by half a poet?

1944

FOR FREEDOM

Look brother, the day dawns!
Look how the edges of the vast dun clouds
Are tipped with silver!
Look how one shaft of light climbs up the sky!
The island stirs and shudders in her sleep
As when within the womb
The enceinte woman feels
The urge and surge of birth.

Lo! the day dawns.
'Twas such a dawning when a century gone
The slave-men were set free,
When fields were cradles rocked with song
And woods were hung with a wild harmony,
And the winds hummed joy's deep intensity.
Now we, the heirs of that first freedom,
Watch in this new dawn
A fuller freedom born.

1944

CARIB AND ARAWAK

Blood red the hedge hibiscus blooms,
Blood red, blood red.
And oh,
The bright stain of the wide petal,
The odourless leaf,
The yearlong blossom,
The flagrant flower,
Oh, the bright stain is the loud blood
Of that wild race,
The first, the fallen,
The angry, the defeated men.

Bright was their blood and bitter
Upon Spanish steel.
On the armouries of Aragon,
On the blue lined blades of Seville.
Earth drank and shrank
Where fury drooped
And where the warm pools clogged cold.
Earth drank,
And oh, the hedge hibiscus blooms
Blood red, blood red.

1945: as Merton Maloney

45

COLOUR (for Harold Telemaque)

The island world is filled
With the sky's blues and ocean's,
With the earth's green and ocean's
The cloud's white and the wave's.
Sunrise is golden fire,
Is crimson and is silver,
Day's light within, upon,
Makes star-dance on the water,
Tipples the waves and leaves,
Makes silver towers of clouds.
Day passing on a pall
Of paling colours, ends
Like embers: Westward is glory.
The earth explodes in colour,
Flames immortal on hill,
Hibiscus great and flagrant.
Gay as a scarlet woman,
Is bright with her abandon,
Poinsettia spreads her crimson,
The poui's crown is golden.
Come painter, come,
Down on the sun's long road,
Down the great rainbow's arch,
Come poet, come,
Up through a chasm of earth,
Up from that darkness
Where life sleeps and dreams,
And breathes her great rare dreams,
Through golden corridors,
Whence their splendours come,
As poets among men.
Come painter, poet, come,
And with the sun's hot ardour,
And with the earth's rich rhythms
Interpret us this beauty.

1947

HURRICANE HILL

As I was walking up Hurricane Hill
Foot after foot up the great green hill
The wind lay down, the wind was still.
And the colour of the sea within my view
Was the colour of the sky, a Titian blue.
And the slow wave laughed on the long shore,
Laughed and returned and laughed the more;
And the wind arose from her evening sleep
And spoke to me in her whisper deep;
"Brother, brother,
Sure as you go, a ghost comes after."

I laughed, my silent easy laughter.
"Oh there are hosts, and hosts and hosts
Of native and forgotten ghosts;
For every man that dies in the land
His ghost roams loose I understand."

"Nay," said the wind, "it is not so,
'Tis hate or love makes a ghost go
Season on season to one place
Like waters in a chasmed race.
'Tis hate or love – a wounded life,
Gives to dull death a deathless strife.
And here's one that follows after
Though you essay your foolish laughter.

"For her love fell down and her love died
With an arrow in his side
When the Spanish bowmen came
And chased him as they chased the game.
Carib he was and Cacique too.
But he fled uphill and in full view
Of the haughty, angry Spanish don
Who lusted his gold and his lovely woman.

"He took her and used her as he willed
Till her strength was drained and her life was stilled:
But he used her dead as men eat meat,
For she was stiff and cold and dead in spirit
That hour her love died on the summit
Of Hurricane Hill
Where her ghost haunts still."

1948

A LOVER SPEAKS

Climb up a rainbow's arch
And be arrayed in all that loveliness;
Be gilded as a sunset cloud
Or take the moon's soft radiance for gown
And the great stars for diamonds,
Be costumed like a queen in cloth of gold
And all the earth's rare and famous finery,
Be what you will for I am fancy free.

Become all legend beauty,
The glorious goddess from Olympus leaping,
Contested Helen or the Pharaoh queen,
Isolde or Deidre,
All that fair company that pass
In love and sorrow down the corridors
Of rhyme and story.
Be what you will for I am fancy free.

But, when your bright imaginings shall end
And you are your black hair,
Black eyes, deep lips and dark complexion;
When you are native to this time and island,
Attractive in the streets and gay and graceful,
Your beauty maddening in the moment's dusk,
Your Naiad nakedness in the clean sea;
When you are you
Then shall my fancy be not free
But slave and bound to what I love to see.

1948

SOUNDS LIVE

Sounds live eternally,
Forevermore wandering
Like ghosts in the gloaming
In the land of their birth.
Hear the far faint echoes
Of Carib arietos
Trailing down
The arches of the dawn.
Hear, softly, ghostly
On the water
Splash of many-oared canoes.

Hear sword-swish
And arrow-swoop,
Hear, echoing from the hills
The cannon anger;
Hear in the wood
And in the bamboo copse
Down by the stream
The sob-end of a scream
Where a man died
Or a maiden:
Hear if your ears will hear.

Hear in the evening rain
The deep drawn sigh of pain,
The weary body's
Shamed resignedness.
Hear what comes after
Weariest laughter:
Woe was not writ in water.

Hear in the old house
The tread of older shoes,
The rustle of old garments
Not in use.
And for the keener ear
Which love has given to hear,
The ghost sound of a kiss
From ghost mouths
That have loved
All this last century
In the ghostly dark.

1948

DUSK

Day is ending
And world greying
As dusk clusters,
But there are hints
Of sunset tints
Of cumuli
Around the sky.

Day is ending,
Clouds are sharing
The sun's gift
With lowlier water,
For on the sea-face
Colour lingers
Like old embers.

Day is ending,
Sea is sighing
And sea gulls wing
Their homing flight
In leaden light,
Their pinions wide
In endless glide.

Day is ending,
Dusk descending:
In wooded dells
With cypress bloom
Adorns the gloom,
The silent angelus
On the hour.

Day is dying
And this ending;
And to the night
For new delight
Will beauty bring
In midmost hours
Thought's lissom powers
And drifts of dreams.

1948

SHE (for Basil Pitt)

She is Caribbean. She is the meaning,
Flower and fruit of our four centuries
Of ruthless traffic, of dark uneasy peace
Among ourselves, of reckless greedy gleaning
From old continents, and the commingling
Of our blood with wanton, lustful ease.
She's Europe, Africa and Asia these
And the native Carib disappearing.
She's beauty set in a rare frame of beauty
Flame-flowered immortelle and flamboyant
Crimson hibiscus and bright golden poui,
Green foliage and sheer blue of sea and sky
Surround her with their loves; they flaunt
The pride and passion kindling in her eye.

1949

THE LEGEND OF ANACAONA

They wrote their names,
Their race, their pride,
Their dancing figures,
Their brief history
On white flats of stone
Planed clean by wind and sunlight;
They added daily to their human record.

In their cacica's chamber
Earth-brown vases
Held her great red roses
Blazing against the sea-green draperies;
Loveliest for the loveliest;
All the best in Xaragua
For Anacaona, cacica, dancer.

But iron vikings
Ravening from the sea
Bawled in the bay
Their battle name.
Their iron devils crashed
And shattered the stone records
And shattered shards of goods and gods
Across the hearths and fields.

Mail clanged and jangled
And arms clashed.
A sword blade shattered
The rose vases;
Petals were spattered
Like blood drops on the draperies.
Gauntletted fingers like talons
Clutched the waiting women;
Black daggers struck.

Anacaona screamed
And fainted and fell down.
Don Fernan laughed
The snarling laughter
Of the mountain lion
On the hills of Aragon.
Don Fernan laughed.
They hung her grimly
On a cold and drizzly dawn.

Her bones are grains of sand;
And the white stones
On which she wrote her beauty
Are lost as her loins
That thrummed love's hot canzones
Among her maidens.

1949, 1955

INVOCATION

Sun of my day make dry,
Make dry the dark green swamps
And sodden marshes of the soul:
Stars of my fate, oh, no more preach
Your prophecies of doom.

Now from my heart draw out the adder's hate
That counts the burning whip-weals one by one;
Unbend my knotted hands and light my eyes
O moon of kindness.

Me, let the circling years,
The flowing winds, the streaming waters
And the patient earth enfold and bless
With equal freedoms and with common love;
The rose of hope grows also in my garden.

O Muse, O Goddess, turn my turbid verse
From sour marshes where the snail, the toad
And the wild dog and scaly snake inhabit
Into fair acres where the pouis bloom
As lavish-golden as your legend hair,
Where willow fingers reap from the wind's lyres
Rich fluent rhythms
That shall nourish these and other years.

1949

MARCH TRADES

Earth leans the arctic
Once more to the sun
As the fond lover
After anger's done
Returns unto the loved one.
In the north temperate zone
Spring is being born;
And in our ever glittering
Torrid centre
The trade winds wake
And shake their mane
On earth and ocean.
Fast flows the long green wave
Hurried by their urge
To crash their flowing strength
On furrowed rock and shoaling sand,
But strong is buttressed
Continent and island,
Sturdier than savagery of wind and sea.

Cumuli are shredded
Into flying fluffs
That scud like powder puffs
Tossed to the gale.
Are riven from the boughs
Leaves ochreous
Of cedar, plum and shrub,
And fronded palms are fretted.
In village dooryards
And in close cool orchards
Perennial hardy mangoes
Bloom thick cream,
But the winds shear them
As they shear the fire from Immortelles

To startle the dark wood,
As they shear sheath from bud
And seed from shattered pod.

Close eastern windows
While the high wind blows
Too wildly in the eaves
And curtains fill like sails
And the rooms fret like cabins
Of gale gripped galleons.
Make all ship-shape
In stubborn Colon's simple way,
In the black slave-trader's way,
In buccaneer and pirate way,
In the sturdy sea tramp's way;
Make all ship-shape,
For here on the rugged map
Of the Caribbean
Hurricane centre shifts across meridians;
Jagged lightnings dart
Thunders roll and roar
Under close cloud ceilings
While barometers lower.
Let all be girt
In sinew, heart and spirit
To take the buffet
And to prosper in it.

1949

SHALLOW UNDERGROUND

Oh, shallow underground
In clay and shale is found
The unhappy skull
That never was hopeful

That the full moon would bring
A season of romancing,
Or that the dragging feet
Should be given to dancing,

Even though the dark wood
And the hopeless blood
Shuddered to the thrums
Of the uttering drums

Makes a long soft screen
Across dusk's greying green
Somebody's blue bush smoke
Like an idiot's joke.

West sky's an ochreous leaf
Where sunset's colour sheaf
With crimson, gold and rose
Was grand and gorgeous.

Eastward, the willow's grace
Across the round white face
Of the first night's full moon
Is gently, sagely written.

Oh, but the heart secure
From beauty's Circe lure;
Surely keep the spirit
From any tenure in it.

Let lovers take their stand
Holding ardent hands
And happy dancing children
Singing in the garden.

This is the halcyon weather
For those whose faery feather
Of hope and love and light
Is not engulfed of night,

Whose banner of pure pride
Is green and flaunted wide,
Their precious ignorance
Buoyed by innocence.

1949

TOKEN

The days are dressed
In glory with remembrance
Of that so broken
And so brief acquaintance;
They keep a lingering
Most adored fragrance.

Whisper to winds and stars
This wide delight:
In the dawn's grandeur
Now transfigured stand
Out of tartarean night
To utter to the sun.
Tell the good earth,
The rocks, the reeds, the trees
All one by one;
And to the wizard laughter of the wave,
On which sun silver
For a gilding gleams,
Reveal, reveal the many visioned dreams.

And know
Before the season's spell is broken
That love has given thee
The ancient token.

1949

THE OLD MAN

The old man is as old,
As old as kingdom come,
So old, his days drum
Muddled in his head,
His sight blurs in the sun.

The old man is as grey,
As grey as Jericho,
Thick white cotton top,
White silken lip crop
And white stubble beard.

The old man has seen,
Has seen and set and sealed
Our century of salvation;
Oh, he is our history's
Sagest contemplation.

The old man is a scroll,
A scroll on which I see
My strong ancestral tree
With roots of iron tapped
To thirsty shale and rock.

But turn, turn the page,
Break from history's limit,
Adventure like Colon
Within the earth's full circuit
Upon an opening ocean

After the present stars,
The bright inviting stars
Gleaming where they stand
Over wave and island,
Wizard to the spirit.

Leave to the worn old man
The hour which time has given him,
Grow myrtle on his grave
In sad kind memory of him,
Let the threnodying willow
Keep a tall legend of him.

1949

OH, NO MORE NOW

Oh, no more now
Ascends the heart
Like the green bough:
No more commands the sun
The rhythm of the blood
Like singing sap in wood.

Fond queen of Ithaca
What were you waiting for?
Did your love's greenness
Petrify yet green
In hope for Ulysses?
Did the black arrow sing
The triumph of sweet spring
To your blood returning?

Lucky Penelope,
Luckier far than I
Who by my green warm sea
Wait ever hopelessly,
Ever more hopelessly.

Through the quarried ear
The casuarinas whisper
To the dried-fruit heart
Rough-wrinkled like
The sea-eroded rock,
"What are you waiting for?
Does the flower come
To the withered stem?
Does the prayer begin
At the prayer's amen?"

1949

STRANGER BEWARE

What is faith? and, What is faithless?
Stranger, you who hold his lover
In the neighbour island yonder,
Lightly turn and fondly ask her.

Lightly turn and fondly ask her
Of the years she shed away,
That she count them day by day
Out of her heart into your hand.

That she count them day by day
As the hoarder counts the treasure,
Gem by gem and coin by coin,
Measure upon precious measure.

If on a coin you see an image
Black as Tartar, sad as Caesar's,
Give it back unto the giver.
What is Caesar's leave for Caesar.

All she is is his alone
Whose dark image her day bears,
In whose heart her every feature
Gleams more sad and bright than tears.

All she is is his soul's own,
All her odd and doubtful beauty
Every turn of mind and bone.
All of her so light and faithless.

All of her his heart has worshipped,
All of her his being adores,
And his love like sleep is timeless,
Passionless like death and endless.

And his love does brood like mountains
All around her and within her,
And his love does flow like fountains
Through the channels of her spirit.

And his love is given you
In the words of her caresses,
In her flowers of desires:
And you feast upon his being
Quivering in love's red fires.

Stranger, beware lest she shall leave you
Gazing in a broken mirror,
Gazing at your own reflection
Unaware that you are there.

1949.

FEBRUARY

Trades ardent from the sea
Laugh among the leaves
And are our lovers' hands
Against our faces.

This is the month we love;
The giant immortelles
Splash fire on the hills,
Hold torches in the dells.

The poui trumpets forth
Her golden semibreves
That break and fail
Against the scattering trades.

The clean-limbed glorisidia
Is in her heliotrope;
The humming bird and bee
Revel in her glory.

In the village dooryard,
In the close cool orchard
The mango sprays her cream
Foam on her mountained green.

Life lolling underground,
Hearing news of spring
Leaps in the floral blood,
Breaks out in beauty dancing;

As broken hopes arise
After a prolonged
Drought season of the spirit
When visions light shamed eyes.

The trade winds blow, and we
In our year long sunny season
as proper farmers tend
Each one his given garden.

The green rains come, and we
Out of our nurtured earth
With hoe and hope and courage
Shall charm high harvest forth.

1950

THE FLOWERING ROCK

In fierce hot noons
Neath homestead trees
Our village girls
Breastfeed their young
Whose cradle is a song,
And in our valley
The stream water croons
Cool rhythms among stones.

Our hearts break not
Though they are ever broken;
A froth of laughter
Tops our sea of sorrows,
Our singing sighs like zephyrs
In night silence:
Our voices bear the tracery of tears,
The burden of their cadence.

Oh, from gaunt rock
As white as sanctity
The lily blooms:
Essence of darkness is
Too pure for fragrance,
The distilled stone,
The still voice of the skeleton.

This is our symbol –
Beauty famous in the slum;
The hungry boy who
Tomorrow shall become
The country's hero;
The black loam bears him,
He breeds recurrent
In our fertile womb.

Day breaks, my darling:
Night, cast with eldritch dreams
Shrinks from these shores,
Light flickers on horizons;
Our souls like sunflowers
Turn toward the dawning:
Our hope begins its orisons.

1950

POEM

He plucked a burning stylus from the sun
And wrote her name across the endless skies
And wrote her name upon the waxing moon
And wrote her name among the thronging stars.

If the pale moon forgets, he will remember.
Lovers remember though love's ghost sigh in the sun
Or whimper in despair in the large dark.

The seas are sorrows
And the seas accept the moon's dark tragedies.
The seas reflect the yearning of the stars.
His heart is weary as the endless seas.

His soul is wearier than the flowing wave,
O dark tide of no hope,
O blood of tears still sings the sun.

No cloud can blind, the memory of the moon
Or blot the legend from the ageless stars.

1950, 1951

ECLOGUE FOR CHRISTMAS

The kings that came to the Birth
The heathen outlanders, stargazers and givers
Are gone and are gone:
Weary of fealty and homage
They have deserted the scene
And the picture is faded and the theme is a legend.
No more their winter adventure,
Riding along roads, by-paths and bridle paths
In mud and in snow,
The beasts slipping and stumbling
And the cameleers cursing:
Nor lying in verminous inns,
Hosts charging high prices for poisonous food
And Circe-eyed women, inviting, unveiled,
And whispering wickedness and groping for gold:
Nor tenting in fields
Where bleak winds swear under the staring stars:
Not this hard journey
Though the calling star is a beacon in heaven,
Though dawn will show them the soul of the world.
They come no more
Though immortality hangs on a word to be said
And a gift to be given:
Their hearts like Herod's
Are crazed to the slaughter of innocent children:
Hunger and bombs are halberds and daggers
To murder the manger, the inn and the town:
Hunger and bombs are the bane of the earth.

1950

DEATH DOES NOT

Death does not erase
The figures left by those
Who in their arithmetic
Were expert at each trick,
Nor does, despite the grave,
Silence our singing love:
If but the record's made
Some ear will hear it played.

Set winds in motion or
Take wing in winds; soar
Like the lean hawk; hover
In beauty or in terror;
How you hang gracefully
Under the dazzling sky
Some gazer's eye will mirror,
Some lover will remember.

O, with the seer's rod, knock
Upon the native rock;
Call forth its limpid fountain,
Or, in contempt of pain,
Sculpture a form of faith
From the stone's dull death,
Make of that totem pole
A symbol of our soul.

Stand at the precipice
At the end of the race;
Pose and leave pictures there,
The last, the best, the rare;
And like fearless diver
Leap into the air;
Plunge graceful as a swan
Into oblivion.

1950

POETS AND PAINTERS

Poets and painters, thinkers, strugglers,
We who endeavour here
To write the future with the fire splendour,
O that we could carve open the stone skull of the dull time,
O that like a boulder
We could carry this odd world on our shoulder.

My father the strong man
Could set his stamp upon
The sterile fields of clay or stone;
With mattock, hoe and spade, the good, couth tools
He wrote his will upon such stubborn earth
And charmed sweet harvests forth.
And are we lesser pioneers than he?

Midnight is struck
And on my eastern hill as pale as mist
The waning moon swims in a sea of mist.
The death within us dies; grief's phoenix sire
Is fagged to ashes in redeeming fire,
And dawn is eager for the thundering wing.

Time is a bomb in the heart;
Now, now, no more;
Tear barriers down, efface the frontiers,
Water the barren plainlands, drain the marshes;
Plough deep in the drought season;
Rich harvests ripen upon nurtured acres;
Cool courage shall confound old griefs and fears.

1950

BEYOND

Beyond the flood of sunlight on this sea,
Beyond horizon line,
Beyond those outer and unknown horizons
Into horizonless and glorious landscapes of the soul
Take wing, take wing; outward go singing.

Not as stark men upon a drowning deck
Or on a berserk salient doomed;
Not as wind-driven wingers crying,
Nor lowing as lost ones from flocks;
Not as the hermit in his cold cell chaunting –
Not these, not these, but the light-throated,
Sun-carolling of the joyous defiant,
The darer in air, the plunger in waters.

Pass over mountains;
Your cadenzas cascading, echoing, re-echoing,
Shall strain dark cataracted eyes
From cabbage beds, from damp potato ground:
They blinking in sun shall remember their youth,
Their glory gone to the midden of years,
Their spearheads rusting.

O, from your eyrie wash them with song
Like sunlight flooding, pouring through doors,
Through last slow closing shutters of the soul.
Wake them to pain, to laughter and to loveliness again;
From the dark vats of grief this century cooling,
Drench them again like rain.

Go on, O singing man!
There are the eagles the great-winged before you
Reigning in sunlight, the hawks and the swallows:
O join them soaring beyond and beyond
Over limitless landscapes!

1950

TRANSITION

Watching my wisp of smoke
I know where our dreams go.
I know how spirit builds
Pylon and pyramid
Needling receding heaven;
How soul the arrower,
Burster of horizons
Goes out like hawk and eagle.
Through the star-cluttered night
I go where my dreams go.

Come dawn, come sun, come cloud,
Bird-talk, cock-crow, dog-bark;
Man slipping in from sleep
As from another journey
Into the inn of day;
Earth turning from nocturne
To morning rhapsody;
My mother island catching
At my heart and feet;
I go where my blood goes.

I go where my love goes;
Where the salt sea sprays
Her salt into the blood;
Where my little river
Runs rhythms out to sea;
Where the green hill's tower
Stands against the sky;
Where in fertile valleys,
Grand, green fields of corn
Preach of splendid harvests.

Here in my huddled village
Blood pulses into blood;
Kinsman halloos kinsman;
Deep-bosomed women gossip
From dooryard into dooryard
And children scamper barefoot.
Ah, there the heart-gold goes
Slender as the young palm,
Comelier than Sheba
Golden in young sun.

1950

FRIGATE BIRD PASSING

Consider here that great hawk arrowing
The rare air, crashing opposing cloud,
His eye needling horizons, iron wing,
Untiring heart, his blood a fountain singing;
For perch upon this sea-ringed rock
Consider his contempt.

Where last did he touch ground?
Feeling the wind in his belly
Over what tableland he floated
Watching the prey that could not flee
His hard down-driven need?
Where stood he gorging red beak and talon
Tearing the still quivering thing?

Then O from there he beat the buoyant wing
And strode with thunder into air,
Attained that altitude
And veering east he grew into our view.

Up there beyond our grounded blood and bone
Only our dreams can reach him
Only the pinioned spirit check his course.
There in his great airfaring
He dips wing only to eagles,
To his wild migrating kin;
Exults in storms
And at wild lightnings screams and hurtles on
Proud in his keen career:
He shrills his epics to the risen sun.

And as I dream my lover in the noon
Divinely kind and soft and warm at dusk,
Or as the holiest picture paradise

Clear at death's distance, island of their God,
So in the inner mirror of his eye he sees
The dazzle of his white Andean perch,
The cruel ice-rind of the wintry pole.

He flies and dreams.
His hard sure instinct beams him on
While steep beneath him sleeps the green sea death
That shall immobilise his viking wing.

1950

BIRTH (For Judith Herbert)

The song from night the mother comes
As from the womb to your morning of being,
A spark from the impact and fusion of loves,
A flame ascending in the passive air,
Beauty rose-opening, a birth taking bone,
You came to become an item of living.

Sweet luck to be flung from an instinct to flame
To an instinct to beauty; to be seed and promise
To a grafting of gifts; to draw from your roots
At the vital and rarest sources of life:
The sun will tell you all his Cancer saga
And swans of your love swim lagoons of the moon.

The magic of songcraft circles your cradle.
Dream, dream clear images. Rhythms hover and beat
On wings in your air and rock you and rock you
In their bosom of tenderness upon chords of creation.
Grow in this ray of my song, my singing this midnight;
I die with your dawn; your noon will not know me.

1951

THE OLD HOUSE

Desolate lawns round a desolate house
That stands in sorrow in the sun
And to the cold heart of the moon
Mourns her own death, her ruined grace.

She tells of all her wasted treasure;
A mellow man, as good as bread,
Sweet as his fruits, husbanded here,
But his are gone and he is dead.

The boy I was ran through these doors.
The house was all over gracious and lovely,
Her folk were brown, rose-mouthed and comely,
Buoyant as birds and birdsong in woods.

The piano's crumbled in the corner,
A broken tomb of old dead tunes;
Their clock's its skeleton; the wind
Breaks through their walls and one door walls.

The loveliest lady of the house
Whose brown hands lovelier than tunes
Made lovely grace notes through tunes
Died and broke the house's heart.

And one is like a stricken swan
Dying in simple silent faith
Within grave white hospital walls,
Deceived by hope the heart conceives.

And one is prematurely grey;
Ground and sifted into griefs
She heaps the dust on the dead day
Weeping her lover cheated away.

She measures indigence in town,
Measures the growing of her sons
Against the slide rule of the years,
Against her beauty wasting away.

La mère seems deathless in her age,
Green in her decrepitude,
Laughing from the skeleton,
Rattling the dead bones of her years.

And I who nourish a rose tree
With blood from vein and artery
Drop down at the rose's root
And give my heart that it may flower

That they may live a poem's age
In the green house a poet builds.
O may they know, who told my youth
To sing and dance, I tell their death.

HOMESTEAD

Seven splendid cedars break the trades
From the thin gables of my house,
Seven towers of song when the trades rage
Through their rich green season foliage.
But weathers veer, the drought returns,
The sun burns emerald to ochre
And thirsty winds strip the boughs bare,
Then they are tragic stands of sticks
Pitiful in pitiless noons
And wear dusk's buskin and the moon's.

And north beyond them lie the fields
Which one man laboured his life's days,
One man wearying his bone
Shaped them as monuments in stone,
Hammered them with iron will
And a rugged earthly courage,
And going, left me heritage.
Is labour lovely for a man
That drags him daily into earth
Returns no fragrance of him forth?

The man is dead but I recall
Him in my voluntary song.
His life was unadorned as bread,
He reckoned weathers in his head
And wore their ages on his face
And felt their keenness to his bone
The sting of sun and whip of rain,
He read day's event from the dawn
And saw the quality of morning
In the sunset mask of evening.

In the fervour of my song,
I hold him firm upon the fields
In many homely images.
His ghost's as tall as the tall trees;
He tramps these tracks his business made
By daily roundabout in boots
Tougher and earthier than roots;
And every furrow of the earth
And every wind-blown blade of grass
Knows him the spirit of the place.

A slave-man's son, a peasant one,
Paysan, paisano, any common
Man about earth's fields, world over
In the cotton, corn and clover
Who are unsung but who remain
Perpetual as the earth winds pass,
Unkillable as the earth's grass:
And from their graves within their graves,
They nourish arteries of earth
And give her substance, give her worth.

O sons, O strong ones from their loins,
Boldly inherit the rich earth
Though you keep their homespun traces
Or run in splendid gilded races.
O poets, painters, thinkers turn
Again and take new craft from old
Worth and wisdom on the wold.
O cornerstones of the crazed world,
O nourishers of earth's best blood
Reclaim the weary dying good.

1951/52, 1958

LETTER TO LAMMING

Older than you and cooler, more content,
I hold my narrow island in my hand
While you have thrown yours to the sea
And jumped for England, where, beyond my gaze,
I hear only your seasonal voice,
A lonely sea gull's crying on Atlantic.

My brother's is an echo's voice,
But love leans out to exile as to love
Lost or to the lately dead;
Forgive the thought divining you unhappy
In the vast alien city,
Aliened by pure prohibited complexion,
Hungry in bone and spirit.

Forgive the dream that drags you back to islands,
Desiring your genius home again
Among the immortelles and poincianas
Dropping red pathos on our naked graves;
Among our peasants barefoot as their cattle
In the intemperate weathers of our days.

Here in my dooryard's naked indigence
Hard labour bruises and lays bare the bone
Bent down for bare existence to the stone.
In shanty towns is hunger, harsh, immoral,
The ladies of the dark parade their ware,
And ulcerous Lazarus groaning in the ghetto
Stodges a filthy offal not for dogs;
Oh for your oratory for the stricken dumb.

Our islands still are greener than we know them,
Our hopes are jungles of quick turbulent growth;
In skulls as fossil as the wrath of slaves
Our ranting politicians pour foul potions

Poisoning the innocent good.
We are enslaved in the ancestral cane,
We're trapped in our inheritance of lust,
The brown boot scorns the black,
And skins not white as white
Deny the black old matriarch in the cupboard.

Does winter prick the marrow as your dreams —
Classic images of hunger dancing
To reiterated rhythms drumming blood,
Hungry children skipping back to school,
Wrinkled and gnarled grandmothers crouched to chores
That children of the prodigal's should eat,
Harsh laughter lapping up the streams of tears —
Do these stark patterns break the estranged heart,
Or does the banked Atlantic mar their passage?

Why were we born under the star of rhyme
Among a displaced people lost on islands
Where all time past is knotted in time present?
Here we are architects with no tradition,
Are hapless builders upon no foundation;
No skilled surveyors mark our forward road.
Can we speed through a score of centuries gone,
Leap from the sheer escarpment of our time
And mount like eagles proud-winged among eagles?

Here by the sea I sweat in prayer for you
Watching your kestral way
Across that sky and climate, man of islands.
Remember cadences of island patois,
Old men goatskin drumming,
Young men's tin percussion,
The sun's rose ruddy in our blood,
The wine excitement of our island women;
O man, your roots are tapped into this soil;
Your song is water wizard from these rocks.

1952

MEN

Ripened in-to man,
Ripening into rhyme,
Feeling a single theme
Insistent in my bone
Knock louder than love's dream,

I hope I'm ripe to write
Perfection in the verse
As I am ripe to die;
That love will squeeze the heart
Till the love's run dry.

Blood will wander where
It must but return home
To the heart's villages
Rickety beneath
Mango and breadfruit trees;

To my darling village
Huddled to my hill,
Where each man to his house
Live my village kinsmen
Subject of my verse.

They are my very bone
Whose rugged strength compels
The stone-song in my blood,
Whose simple speech dictates
Rough rhythms to my head.

They are not brilliant men
Or hot heroic men,
Only broad homely men,
Common labouring men,
Barefoot, earthy men.

Yet these are they on whom
Brave empires are founded,
But when proud purple's dust
Their common blood continues
Deriding glory's rust.

Here and all world over
They have been and are
Since man's wisdom's birth
In the earth's green cradle
Man's marrow bone of worth.

These stubborn uncouth bones
Were stones to an infamous house
That time indignant broke
From its clay foundations
Stroke on righteous stroke.

Their stone-hard dooryard earth
Is hallowed with slave blood
That died this century gone
And shudders in the earth
Aphonous as stone.

And yet they are not bitter
Or rebellious men,
But like an old deep river
Quiet to the eye
Are calm in every weather.

They will go on forever
These tough resilient men
Who strive with hoe and shoulder
As brothers to the ox
To break bread from the boulder.

They pit against the earth
In drought and in rain season
Their instinct and their science;
The saga of their sweat
Grows out of each crop's sentence.

Calendars of weathers
Phases and moods of seasons
Are legend in their lives,
Lodged in their slow blood,
Go to their unnamed graves.

For the living and the dead
I scrawl an autograph
In my untutored rhyme;
I spell an epitaph
On the marble-stone of time.

1952

TREE

Her flowers are gone and all her boughs
Are arching with maturing fruit;
She chants magnificats to sun,
Proclaims her worth in motherhood,
Proclaims perpetual fruitfulness of earth.

Serves me for symbol; green years gone,
Love's petals scattered, out of season,
And the blood's fire burning down
I stand up siring my song
Conscious of the pride and poise of fullness.

I spearhead the nigger hope.
I am the first slave's shattered dream
All ever crushed beneath the boulder,
The accumulated mountained prayer
Of the wrecked, wretched generations dead.

Regard me stalwart in the sun;
My hope is founded on the granite
Rock of desolation; my bone
Holds strength from stubborn slave endurance;
My soul is unwound from the iron wrong.

I have grown taller than my pain
As trees outstrip the crowding shrub
Striving for room for light like love
To spread, to build their verdant boughs
Into the benediction of the trades.

I reach to ripeness on my rocks.
O world, take honey from my worth
Or wine or wisdom, mirth or song
Or simple nourishment like bread
Or tap my ample heritage of strength.

Draw on my reservoir of hope:
I do not grow like candles burning
Down into the soulless dark:
I am my rooted symbol tree
That comes to stature and to fruit and ripeness.

The years shall wind away the leaves
Till the tree stand bare of bough,
Stripped of green pride, despair, hate, rage;
Nor ever contradictory weathers
Nor the mad winds shall break the tall stark tower.

And if one single bird descend
Blind with delight and love and faith
A reed upon the tempered wood,
And sing and sing till it drop dumb,
None, none shall mourn what's passed till song is done.

1952

SOMETHING SEEN

Something seen or heard or known long ago
Or something done returns into the heart;
Some image out of childhood comes to mind
Husked, clean and clear that was not understood;
Word, look or scene or thought or circumstance
Comes prodigal again into the heart.

A scene I saw today uproots the past
That lay bone-quiet in its grave of years:
Three women hoeing on a hillside field,
A green and terraced acre of potatoes,
An emerald page in the midmorning sun
On which the past lay printed like a poem.

The strong men whom I honoured as a boy
Made heavy hired labour in the fields
In the sun's blast, soaked in their nigger sweat
And neither they nor I on that day knew
Them deeply cheated of their drudgery's worth:
Freedom's reward to slavery's wretched heirs.

They were the children of slave ignorance
And challenged iron labour with tough bone
Selling their needy freedom to the greed
And the wolf cunning of the unscrupulous skin
Without an evil passion in the heart,
With nothing in the heart but the vast void.

Join this sad image to a word I heard
Out of a mouth worth blooding with a blow:
"Teach niggers Latin to lose good cheap labour?"
I neither wept nor raged but something died
And something burst to retching gall in me
To join my dolour to the word I heard.

This pattern is resolved by brutish minds:
Slave mart and pen, man's animal existence
Now beaten down and buried in our ground
Were resurrected on their day of death
And fleshed again in ill-paid large-tasked labour:
The loud luck plundered in our vale of sweat.

A bitter fruit will ripen on our tree
Poor minds left in deliberate neglect
Like soil untended, choke with vulgar weeds
Of kindling anger hate and wild revenge,
Will snarl and roar for justice and reprisal
Till blood dries rabid on the emerald leaf.

Nor beauty, worth, nor human wealth can flower
In this antinomy of seasons, this
Deliberate cleavage of the island climate:
Roll by and laugh in your luxurious car
While I feet cracked and charred in sunburnt dust
Spit angrily behind you and curse out
To curdle up the pink and white complexion:
Volcano, hurricane and earthquake wait.

Something seen or done or known long gone
Comes into mind; some memory of history
Like a legend's moleculed in the blood;
Some law or force of life here activates
Slave generations. Freedom is not a word;
Is not the loss of bondage but the stature,
The growth of the free spirit from the dust,
The dream of justice, dignity and fames.

1952

HAITIAN TRILOGY

I: BLACK GODS

The serpent set to sea
After the exiled,
Swallowing those
Living and dead
They jettisoned on voyages
Along Equator where Atlantic boils;
He crawled like seaweed up the verdant island.

Cock waking crowed at dawn,
The serpent laughed,
Goats bleated noons
He darted his forked tongue
Tasting blood in the familiar voices.
Drum pounded, he lay down,
Sure of satiety in the sacrifice.

Da! Damballa Ouedo!
Papa Legba! Frieda Dahomin O!
Ogun Feraille! You come?
Pound drum! Pound drum!
Ouedo! You see this shame?
Ogun! Give sword! Give sword!
We give you blood!
Petro!

Houngan O! Papaloi!
Aie Mama Samba!
Ah, ah Boukman!
Ah Makandal!
What Ouedo say?
The serpent gone?
We go die in shame?
Dahomey dead?

Then the gods thundered.
Their anger rent the skies
In a rain season of the loas' weeping.
The serpent darted rage,
Hate changed his skin,
Blood blinded him.
The serpent crowed in the red fires
Of the cane acres,
Through the crescending drums.

The loas were furies whirling in the fires;
The Rada revelled in a race of blood.
Dahomey conquered;
The green land drinks peace.
Da sleeps in Eden round the tree of life.
The cock and goat again his sacrifice.

II: BLACK KINGS

That berserk bravery of maddened men,
That terrible antiphony
They drummed their noon of history
Is silent now, is quieted
Dust, ashes in memory.

They raged like tigers, ravening
Through rabid frenzied hate
To a mangled victory;
On jagged peaks of fate
They put on purple empery.

In green innominate earth
The murdered cannot rest;
The tiger's throbbing vein
Burns from his bitter dust
His passion and his pain.

Henri, a hurricane at heart,
Up-hurled his passionate spirit
To crown the clouded mountain
Where only the staggering frigate
And eagle dare attain.

The stone tower is overgrown,
The sword and sheath together
Rotted in graved time,
The crown like the shed feather,
The singer and his rhyme.

Break up the drums, end the wild dance,
The drummers' fires are cold;
Day rays the blood-red wood.
Night's dark rage is rolled
With loa and loud god,
With blood in bloody earth,
Springing rose petals forth.

III: A TEAR FOR TOUSSAINT

Grief freezes the gone year,
Woe the dead winter
Round the dungeoned death
Forbidden to hope's sun.

That woe froze out his breath.
His wide horizon closed
In to wrecking rocks
That foundered his whole hope.

Crashed hurricanes of hate,
Whirled and swirled thick smoke
Of fired towns and acres,
Fell the blind rain of blood.

History reproaches those
Who yoked rank pride and lust
To a gross sovereignty,
Mangled green freedom's boughs.

They trampled with jackboots
Her green fruit on stones
In demented frenzy;
But history hounded them,

Wrecked their rage and riot,
Their fierce rogue usurpation.
They are lost as fools
Ruined with stones they reared.

Their wild fires are ashes
Scattered by time's wrath.

1953

DESPITE ANCESTRAL RAPE

Despite ancestral rape
And the yoked years bowed down with burdens;
Despite miscegenation forced on matriarchs,
And a tall century twisted with our suffering,
We thank our thick Caribbean stars for roofing.

Our eyes are wide;
Our village grips the hill,
Clings rickety to rock and laps the sea,
Whose salt breath blacks bare boards,
For no paint peels where no paint was.

We creak and groan when the Trades gale;
We know that hurricanes will grind
And sweep us to the angered sea;
But how shall men escape God-wrath
Who have no life in God-oblivion?

Feeling the sun-glance livid in our veins
We live in his insistence,
Though our issue is sun-clothed
And our spare earth but barely blunts our hunger.
We have the moon for dessert
The stars are sweets,
And the whole sky is Christmas tree at Christmas.

We scotch the rock for foothold and foundation,
We furrow slopes and terrace rasher steeps
And stand on hilltops hungering to horizons;
Far out our cockle boats insult Atlantic;
We dare, we know we dare the uncertain ocean
As we coerce the earth
And hazard with hard time for richer futures.

We hazard, for the sun incenses,
The stars excite our hopes,
Incite imaginations and the moon
Compels like tides our ignorant blood;
We must ascend the rainbow road
And ride like frigates the adventurous trades
Or die, or die,
But stars are not sad candles for the dead.

1955

I WALK ABROAD

I walk abroad in my fierce July noon
Desiring no shade;
Grown up through morning growing hot
I am inured to my flame fahrenheit;
Heat is my fate;
Drought crowns the hilltop of my day.

This is my own.
I join my voice to the frog-throat in the pond,
To cricket shrill and bird cry in the wood;
I sign my name upon the papyrus
Of plantain leaves broad in my garden,
I'm halo'd with the sun.

This is I.
Under my dazzling skies in my day's fullness,
Under my African transplanted skin
I take Caribbean nature,
Under my continental negroid hair the skull
Assumes the infinite variety, shapes and moods of islands.

I have forgot the depths and dreams of rivers
In a long endless land.
Living on littorals like gulls, almost amphibious,
The sea tides in my blood,
Suns rise and set upon my sea horizons.

I sign upon my hills;
The pen slips down the slopes,
The ink streams out and stains the native sea.
Who holds me to these accidental rocks?

If I go out as I came in, across Atlantic,
Become adventurer, world will know me
Feeling my footsteps on the latitudes,
Clocking my cadence down the long meridians.

1955

NEW YEAR POEM FOR CECIL HERBERT

To be silent in our silent air
Is suicide; we're given speech.
Was ever dawn bird never sang?
Did ever season murder song?

Blind Homer took his drip of gift
Nursing it from rill to river
Then poured out each single drop
To nourish time, fill every cup.

Did any get more gifts than one?
Shake down the golden bough of song
And what had Shakespeare, Milton, Keats
Or good John Donne or William Yeats?

Consider Michael Angelo
Storming his spirit into form,
Storming his heart out upon stone,
Wearing his worn flesh to the bone.

Revisit Van Gogh, mad, at Arles,
And Gauguin sickening in the sun,
And Chopin fashioning life long
Tall immortality in song.

The dead are in the audience yet,
The laurelled dead. They see us all
Through the hawk's eye of the Giver;
They toss contempt upon the waster.

Did ever season murder song?
Our slave grandmothers in the sun
Wearied and broken to the bone
Chanted their dolour and are gone.

And we the laughers from their loins
In ignorance of their mortal pains,
Are wasters of their wounds and worth
To choke the fountain welling forth.

Consider we construct for sons
A roof of weathers to their gains;
Heirs of the first adventurers
Are no more the pioneers.

Each in his climate, artist, sage,
Adorns his time with act and thought;
The gazer and the listener
Applaud the wonder in the air.

The day is still appropriate;
The stage is set, the audience waits;
Time never lets the curtain down
On poet, pundit, hero, clown.

The drum that's throbbing in our bone
Is silent in the skull o' the drone.
The sun that dazzles in our head
Is darkness to the living dead.

1953

CARIBBEAN CORONATION VERSE

The ways were rougher in the island kingdom
When Shakespeare cut and chiselled at his verse,
And Marlowe, martyred in a brawling tavern
Was made immortal by the kiss of death,
His bright blood streaming in the firmament.
Royal and arrogant in London town
Personal as love, desirable as gold,
In her gummed ruffles majesty was woman.

The kingdom was the sovereign's private fief,
The poniard was sharp private enterprise
And the long sword the prized inheritance.
Rough lord and bully villein fitted ship
And manning her with cannon slipped to sea,
Intrepid tourists on a tropic cruise.
Then it was Westward Ho! Hulls through Colon's
Horizons and – Drake's down in Nombre Dios.

John Hawkins pounced upon a continent,
Kidnapped the native in his paradise
And middle-passaged for the Spanish Indies
Smacking the face of trades; bartered and sold
And sailed home sinking with rich merchandise,
The famous pioneer of the three-way passage,
The great slave-trading corsair gentleman
The queen acclaimed him with the accolade.

Exploring all horizons, in bays and estuaries
They planted empire and reaped blood-red adventure,
Bloodstained gold and tarnished honour. Their lustre
Shone and starred their fall on frantic frontiers.
They built their empire for a monument
To their heroic bones. Their arrogance
Crowned cities older than their own. They held
Old glittering dynasties in iron grip.

One other woman's beauty graced the realm
While her great clock rang arrogant noonday round
Her subject world. The lion stalked the sun
And roared rough thunder upon history
That chronicles. The crown was edited
Through kinder years by freedom-minded heirs
Of men who'd set it rough on serf and slave.

They shaped it lovelier to their own proud love
Till now my nigger voice from the slave islands
Proclaims her majesty in Shakespeare's tongue
To queen a commonwealth of flowering freedoms.
Advance Britannia. The prouder empire waits
The valiant spirit's pioneering faith.
In charity to every lesser hope
Democracy be large; be critical
With proper parliaments; crown justice sovereign
As the queen, as evident as suns,
Impersonal and equal each meridian.

1953

IN MANGO SHADE

Here, rotting in my eyot in Atlantic,
Reckoning, idiot, the running tides,
Counting the green pulse of my torrid weather,
Washing my heart in arrogance of colour,
Rhyming rondeaus in mockery of my hope
Knocked to a springing effervescent drum
Trapped in a mirage of my sun-god's eye,
In mango shade I make a trek of dreams.

Somewhere is always noon; place, time, event
Reaches a midday in history high with pain.
It is not difficult to find again
The equatorial road through trade and doldrum,
The ancestral shadow shortened underfoot
Of anguish, shame, despair and naked fear;
It is not difficult to exercise
Bewilderment and hate and grief and rage.

With noon's flame fallen into afternoon
On islands, slack shadows fall on canes;
Anger is mocked, intensity is stored
To stale, to sour to vintage vinegar;
Truth in my calypso is out of tune;
I am to hum a foreign cansonet;
My drums that summoned my dark voodoo gods
Thrum in the frippery of the carnival.

The noon is twilight: nothing is plain,
Whole, naked, clean; nor do ghosts walk;
The day is parodied; sweat's but a stain
Or, if you will, a mere pastiche of pain.
Art is gone back to heaven or gone to ground,
An eyeless annelid moling in the dark,
To kitchens, pantries, pots and pans, housewives,
Needles, pins and cushions, pinafores.

I say to my heart: Be gay, be gay. Weep not
My heart, I say. Be anonymous, be
The pliant clay in the soil's breast; be
The dough of the bread of life and death. You do
Not know if hopes ever colour like roses, nor when
Doom returns to the nigger between Cancer
And Equator. Consider Jomo Kenyatta
And Malan's mess in his apartheid yonder.

No, no. Do not break the tides of your tears
Upon the reef of the world. Do not despair
Wanderer on island landscapes, perpetual exile,
Leaser of history's goodwill, sharecropper, squatter
On feudal acres; but keep love's light alive
In the private heart; in the spirit's tower the beacon;
Beneath the bone, behind the old rock face
Pray for the grace of the fountain aching from stone.

Pray to preserve the centuries we slaved
A sacred arras of ancestral story.
The pyramids remain, and the taled trek
Through thirst and sea, the legend rustless as faith.
Our feet are deep in slave-despairing ground,
Firm as the cross on Golgatha. The soil is fed
From good spring waters of the human spirit.
First crop's the bitter vetch and the black thorn,
But after, if love plough, shall come
The Christ-sweet bounty of the lovely corn.

1953

109

LEGEND OF DAAGA

The stone preserves the taste of the spent blood.
Child, innocent of history, bystander,
Unaware of the unwritten hieroglyph,
Uncarer, foreigner, ignorant of grief here,
The waves' despair, the threnody of streams,
Listen one moment to the rock-breaker,
The recreator, the reteller of legend.

Stand anywhere you are on any street,
Hill, field or in your quiet house,
And question the fossil inhabitant
Of gone time upon your storied place,
The aphonous bone, history's abiding witness;
Lean ear into the murmuring fountain
Of felled blood, meter the scalding anguish.

Hearing of Daaga from a laughing man
I summoned that dead hero from time's shade
And blessed his savage pride that could not let
Him slave down the tall years when kraal and kingship
Awaited him and velvet love under
Large velvet moons and violent drums incensed
Black valorous hearts and swords and assegais.

He could not slave; his soul would not be yoked
Nor his eyes broken nor his fires quenched.
He could not be quelled to grind the cane.
The wild bull from his bonds bellowed for freedom
To the frantic herd and they fled east
Toward their Africa till the walled sea
Rolled their desire back upon the land.

The angry jungle hunted them in frenzy.
Revengeful boughs screamed in their wild pursuit.
Guns cursed them, swords slashed at their attempt.
Their fallen anguish raved from reeking wounds.
They said: These men must die. Daaga must die.
They built their fatal square of men and guns.
All the high noon the drums crescended death
Whose imminence could not corrupt him.
His pride was a black column in the sun.
The guns saluted his contemptuous heart.

Oh, resurrect the legend from the soil
And see his courage statued in the sunlight
And feel his spirit solider than granite.
I stand to say he's fed my hungry love
And given a stature to my hollow clay.
In the song's womb the hero is reborn,
The slave-bones dance to freedom's singing drum.

1953

POEM

Pray that the poem out of nowhere come
Like the clear fountain jetting from the stone,
Like blossom breaking from the blossomer
And go with grace of clouds under blue heaven,
And sing like light dawn's silver villanelle;
Pray for one phrase from the free elements.

Praise out of heart her whole and hybrid beauty
Now, while the bone stands up, knowing upstanding
Beauty of boughs blossoming to flame and flames
Leaping and falling in fields, on hearths, in hearts
Tender and kind in their first fountained love;
O know her rose among the season's roses.

A viking roving from his temperate island
Greeted Equator where the fanatic sun
Flung darts of torrid light against his eyes
And a dark torrid passion pierced his heart
While dark flame whirled among the jungled drums:
Their seed was flung on islands under Cancer.

Not the gross cunning of the Doric stone,
Those flanks and breasts amazing gods and men:
(That form was cut for a coarse artisan
Who was half-blind from soot in the black forge.)
But the dancer in dreams, Cyprian in tides
Fresh from the seafoam or gleaming at Paphos, goddess,
Goddess, born and reborn, eternally woman,
Eternally loved. Goya had his duchess;
Abelard prayed his sin round a swan's neck;
Lancelot and Tristan drank dark dolorous wine
From golden beakers through audacious days;
And think on Shakespeare's monumented beauty;
On Parnell's passionate wreck; on poor John Keats;
And think on Yeats – the poem's gone to stone.

THE FIGHTERS

We were thrown down upon our blood and bone,
Stone heaped on broken stone in alien acres
Of these western shires; all our inheritance
Was man's first heart, its springing blood,
Its ever springing hope; its greed to eat
Green courage of the careless sun; its lust
To drink to drunkenness of the moon's wine:
O our poor heart that sprung griefs to green rhythms.

But men grow tall through fighting; our anger and
Our hope attacked that wall which fear and fools
Have built between two skins and fanatic pride
Rebuilds where it is worn and cracked and crumbled.
Some Samsons of our strength poised pride and sinew
And challenged skill and won, and growing skilled
And bitter in their pride struck out again,
Till fame brewed tragic ferment in their blood.

Princely and gentle as Sir Lancelot,
Great Peter Jackson fought until he fell
A mockery of himself among the worst
Who mocked him. He died alone, dreaming of greatness.
Sam Langford was one such. He smashed the arch
Of hate; set up old chivalry foursquare
Again in the heroic square. They said
He was the one true negro gentleman.

Jack Johnson stood, with vengeance the black stone
Gripped in his fists. Too angry for his race
Great fame defamed him. He killed with contumely –
The murdering punch and the coarse jeering word.
Rancour brought no redress; but old and blind,
Rotting in garrets, he heard of Joe the tiger,
Stealthy and silent, stalking the arena
He smiled in the cold dark and fell asleep.

I claim their strength and their affranchised pride,
Reopening stubbornly the dead well
Of history of our wretched race that fell
Through utter hell to man's last degradation.
Deep down in the deep seam the water's clear
And clean from the black rock of Africa.
There are bards there and craftsmen, heroes, kings,
And dark ecstatic dancers throng the kraals.

O come my spirit from the rancorous dark
Into the bounty of the human air.
Painter, sculptor, poet in whom the seed
Takes leaf and the leaf greens and flowers like fire,
Speak for the old slave hosts; speak out for us
Who are their heirs, griefs molten from their loins.
Persist to sheer perfection in the work
Like those who pit their perfect and tough sinew
Against arrogance and hate; art, intellect
May scale the granite wall or tear it down.

1953

A DIRGE FOR A DEAD POET

Night dies on my meridian
And time leaps in the gulf
Of dawn where phoenix day
Colours to roses while my grief
Flows like a slow wave in the bay.

O earth, O sun-bound
Wanderer, maker and wrecker
Of burning dreams and bones;
Down-bringer of the skier,
The winged one among the stones;

I heap my ashen griefs,
Dry tears on the sun's altar
Till time's Trade Winds the mound
Of my days' dust shall scatter
Like Troy, like love into your ground.

But not my unfulfilled
Living I mourn here
In these dry cadences,
My unended dying, my clear
Seen destiny time labours, dances.

No, but the young man dead
Who crowed his cockerel light,
Pouring bright poems through
The heavy air, bright,
Jewel bright as crystal dew.

He lived half mortally;
An arrowhead of God,
A star clove through his soul;
He was a prophet's rod
Blossomed, a humming totem pole.

O, and a bounding stag
Hounded in beauty past
Fields, farms, fences
Till the dog's tooth rent at last
The temporal arteries.

Let us salute this death
With the great gone who laboured
To leave gifts in colour,
Form, song or a splendour
Of images; name him in man's honour.

1954

THE WHITE COFFIN
(For Jean Herbert)

Move among the mourners, the heart
Shut dark in the bright afternoon,
Mutter the common stupidities,
But say in the dry oasis of your being:
The commonplace recurs, it's a child's turn.

Hear the words of the wicked man,
The preacher, faith long denied him,
Groping in the darkness of this death
And in the marrow of our human darkness,
The void and hopeless core of the soul's cold: ˙

"The first things are passed away."
Oh, all our youth, the hope and the heaven
Are gone into graves deeper than this girl's,
Blacker than her mother's mourning,
Our faiths died in man's worst famine.

Oh, we are old, our hopes are greyed
To the whiteness of her coffin;
Yet our eyes mirror beauty
And our bodies feel the shudder of begetting,
Ploughing and planting life to our going.

"The first things are passed away."
Tell from the first death, of mothers
Sprouting the seeds of their blood,
Generation on generation, like recurring corn
In the rich earth of their loin's love:

Tell of the girl and her first gift
Of flesh, and the sprung seed filling
To burst from the womb, and this death's
Waste of all that beauty, all that nurture
And the woe of the stone returned to the womb

Of the heart before noon.
O what shall burst love's tomb of pain?
The seal of death is never broken.
The stone will never be rolled
From the sepulchre of grief.

"The first things are passed away."
The hymning children call to cherubim
Through this mourning air. Shall she dance
In Eden? This coffin would flower;
The dead would break their bones for bread
And offer their blood for our faiths
And light the world with their candle of Christ,
For they know our night, our famine and fear
As we crouch under the volcanic sun.

1954

LADY BY THE SEA

(For Maeve Elliot)

Lodged over and against the sea
You hear continually her grief and rage
Continually your heart is chasmed to her passage,
Her pouring through the arteries of your being,
The bay of your dwelling.

She is the blood's source taste and the lymph's look;
Beauty's her daughter, that most beautiful one,
That goddess, the eternal woman
Who walks within men's dreams,
Tragic and lovely as her mother the sea
Century after century.

Your ocean knows the folktale of our grief.
We groaned in her green jaws
Passaging in Trades in a crazed time,
In the tiger's yawn of the torrid doldrum;
We had not dreamed such waters
Who had known only rivers, torrents
And the land mammoth, mountainous
Or rolling out beyond the heart's horizons;
But earth stood up for us,
We crawled out upon islands
And leeched again like trilobite to rock.

Shames were our household goods,
And our gods fled,
And our speech stumbled to silence
On these parishes our hearts hold now
With love green as the landscape,
Peopling the archipelago with hope.
That love or this sad death:
The beached shell weeping its dry tears,
Continually echoing the dead sea.

Look, beauty burns:
Scape and flower delight the child and stranger;
The cloud swims in the wind, wind in the light;
The sea around us, the dark womb of earth,
Eternity is fluid, constant, terrible
And splendid beyond all feeling;
And you, our lady, looking on the sea,
The black rose our blood bears out of its fortitude,
Century after century.

Each rock, each pastoral green scene
Ate yesterday's passover,
Sees history writing down our stress and anger,
Nursing tomorrow's foetus in her womb,
Knowing the torrid tones of the harsh zone.
We build, build hearth and temple,
Plant, pray for harvest,
Our roots prospect for water.

Blood grows and blooms:
One hand may disinter
All the folkfaces stationed in the stone;
One mind may knead the nation's
Till each island eat one large philosophy;
One poet's dream may join the people's
And rejoin the wind and sun and sea,
Flowering and fruiting like a tree
Century after century.

1954

AT GRAFTON BAY

A greenery of arching fronds
Tops these littoral palms;
Soft breezes stir a susurrus in them,
But high seawinds tease and torment them
Tossing their columns under the sky.
Their green round chalices of fruit
Hold bread and wine of earth and sun,
A sweet cool eucharist for all.

The tide rolls foam into the bay,
And with the wind speaks in the scene
Hear as you may what other voices:
Through wind and water, faith and prayer,
Whisper of growth and cloud's soft drifting,
The glittering melody of light,
The lyric of each wheeling world,
The epic of the universe.

Rooted in sand, long ropes to the sea
Reap the bones of the sea; rope-tough
Sinews, Peter's and all, hauling at ropes.
For a seacatch of Christ, for the meal of a miracle
Multitudes hunger, for peace on the waters.
The shoal of life drowns in the air
Till the fullness of death, the stillness of rock
Possess and restore them, sepulchre from pain.

All's relative, reciprocal;
Death scythes down the sinewed reapers;
Lo, they fall to earthen bins,
To the bitter shark-tooth burial;
Their dole of labour, hunger, pity
Stumbles on empty tragedy;
The ceaseless, ruthless sullen sea
Snarls at their rock of destiny.

1954

FOR THE PEASANT PEOPLE OF THE ISLANDS

Despite ancestral rape,
The years of the dead slave,
The breaking of our breed,
Humility, disease,
Hunger, we're home again
Upon the shoal of islands.

We know well what we are;
Our hovels lean to hills,
Tilt like cranes in swamps,
Are rickety on rock
Beside the mocking sea
That spits on our bare boards.

We groan when the Trades gale;
Hurricanes will wreck us;
But when September comes
We pray, and if storm comes
We suffer but we meet
Christ on each storm crossed street.

The sun yawns in our loins.
Our naked children grow
Awry without milk,
Laggard from starch and dirt.
They get the moon for toy,
Stars for their Christmas tree.

We terrace the steep hills
For yam and corn and bean;
From hilltops see horizons
Gleaning the sea's grain
As we coerce the earth.

Cramped in the narrow room,
The torrid littoral,
The prison of the spirit,
Winds call the young away
From hovel, hut and cottage,
From the open door;
But where they go they take them,
Theirs for ever more.

1955

BALLAD OF CANGA

Canga Brown is coming down
Stilted on his legend
Taller than a tall man
Living beyond his end.

He is a old Ashantee man
Full of wickedness;
Bring obeah straight from Africa
What he curse don't bless.

They gang him in the cane field;
Wouldn't raise a straw.
"Get up and work old man; look sharp,"
"Work is not for Canga."

They tie him to the whipping post
In the greathouse yard;
Big whip peeling off his back.
The missis bawling hard.

Canga working obeah bad,
Throwing all the pain
Hotter than he get it
On the baccra woman.

They let him go and chase him
To maroon in the bush.
"Go you worthless nigger,
Let hungry eat your flesh."

But Canga go and sit down
By a tamarind tree,
Beat drum and call Damballa
Till his belly hungry.

He plant a plantain sucker.
Fill a tub with water
Fish mullet from the water,
Cut plantain in one hour.

When moon go down old Canga
Put his skin in a jar,
Fly in a ball of fire:
Man turn soucouyan!

He suck the white man blood
Till his flesh come dry.
Only three days later
The man lay down and die.

He suck the baccra breeding sow
Till the hog come lean.
"Ent this hog was making pig?"
"Everyone gone clean."

What give Canga Brown that power?
He don't eat salt nor sugar;
His flesh fresh like Ibo yam,
His blood like clean rain water

The devil come for Canga
Riding four black horses;
But Canga make black magic
And turn to two jackasses.

"Canga Brown! Ba Canga O!"
"Where the old man gone?"
Jackass braying loud like hell
Behind the baccra barn.

When God come for the man
And call him: "Canga, Canga."
That old sinner tie his mouth;
Not he, he wouldn't answer.

God stretch out his crookstick:
"Sinner, get up, go down."
"Look, if I going up or down,
Lord, call me Mister Brown."

God vex until he laugh in heaven;
Pull a big chair for Canga.
Is that why when the man dead
You hearing so much thunder.

TROY WORLD

A rancorous blood, a common, levelling,
Iniquitous, boisterous blood floods on the world;
Wisdom is ruined; the sceptre and the orb
Of golden rule are snouted into dust;
Between the rumble of the herd and legion
The great of heart are trodden on and broken.

A town fell down for Leda's daughter; beauty
Too hot for men's hands burnt out man's hope
To rubble and ashes; all their future was martyred.
For us who burn now on the bough of time
A cold harsh lust wields hammers of fire
And the kingdom of man totters on Abaddon.

Ascend the mountains loveliest of orators;
Call the earth-folk from fields, factories, furnaces,
Warrens of cities; still the blind sea of wrath;
Cleanse us of blood; break the brown bread of peace,
The Eucharist that rots under the stone
Of the heart of man who starves and swallows his fear
And crouches with the sun a sword in his hand.

1955

HAWK HEART

I take this tree for symbol,
These barked and leafless branches stark
Against the noon-glazed, glittering sky.
So man, the blood's pride done,
Broken the structural skeleton,
Cold in the old cold rock;
Lo, all the generations downed
Mould-coffined, mute as stone,

Barren as sand, though even they lie
In marble or in lapis lazuli.
Only our rarest dance, flower,
Sing, ring golden bells of beauty,
Wisdom, wander where they will.
The hawk's heart and the hawk's rage
Possess them; they whirl up
In powerful spirals from their roots.

Oh, may the sun burn open cages
Of my being, heal my halt hope.
Hawk my desire past horizoning islands
To cry world over wisdom's words,
A tempest to the spirit, beating
Rank darkness back, a fire to crack
Man's winterfall of fear,
And recall pentecostal spring.

1955

THE BLIND WEAVERS

I run to your roof from the rain
You hear dampening December;
I call you greeting to startle
Your blind weaving,
To flutter the light at the heart of your dark.

I should be Jesus of miracles
Thinking you pity; but how
May the blasphemous passionate man
Give eyes of his dark,
The light of his world of his rage and his lust?

I know the world of your loss.
I range a blind field
For a bough of laurel
To wear in my hair,
To wear on my grave in the rock of the land.

Blind Homer, blind John Milton
Are my masters. Could I,
As from their dark, they told
Faith, beauty, deeds,
I should grow taller than the timber.

They are taller than time.
Their hair catches the light-cast
On clouds. Their proud poems
March with immortal
And majestic tread
Through each applauding generation.

1955

TO MY MOTHER

It is not long, not many days are left
Of the dead sun, nights of the crumbled moon;
Nor far to go; not all your roads of growth,
Love, grief, labour of birth and bone
And the slow slope from the blood's noon
Are shorter than this last.

And it is nothing. Only the lusty heroes
And those whose summer's sweet with lust
And wine and roses fear. The children do not;
Theirs is young Adam's innocence.
The old do not; they welcome the earth's suction
And the bone's extinction into rock.

The image of your beauty growing green,
Your bone's adolescence I could not know,
Come of your middle years, your July loins.
I found you strong and tough as guava scrub,
Hoeing the ground, reaping the ripe corn;
Kneading and thumping the thick dough for bread.

And now you're bowed, bent over to the ground;
An old gnarled tree, all her boughs drooped
Upon the cross of death, you crawl up
Your broken stairs like Golgotha, and dead bones
Clutch at your dying bones...

I do not mourn, but all my love
Praise life's revival through the eternal year.
I see death broken at each seed's rebirth.
My poems labour from your blood
As all my mind burns on our peasant stock
That cannot be consumed till time is killed.

Oh, time's run past the time your hands made bread
To this decrepitude; but in the stream
Of time I watch the stone, the image
Of my mother making bread my boyhood long,
Mossed by the crusty memories of bread.
O may my art grow whole as her hands' craft.

1955,1957

DOGGEREL FOR ADOLESCENCE

I wave my hand, wish you good day
And wish you luck along your life,
As I pause upon the street
And watch you walk to womanhood.

You laugh above your jutting breasts
Half in innocence and instinct
That I see your bud of beauty
Bursting on the old rose tree.

I know you for this season's song
As you flex your April flesh
In the cunning taunting rhythms
Of the sleek cat and her kind.

O, did the wondrous Nefrete,
The clay complexion on the Nile,
So incense her age's sun
And so outrage the raging moon?

I ask the great tree time herself,
The legends growing evergreen.
They do not say. How then can you,
The innocent doe in the old wood?

I smile again because I know
The heart is lost to touch the stars,
And like the rosebud folds on love;
But O my dear and O my dear,

You'll know the irony of noon,
How like a child does innocence
Cry lost among the naked crags
And dreams migrate into the moon.

Go your great ways, dance all along
In your proud pose, lovely and brave,
Awakening Eve, each goddess young;
You are all men's greener dreams.

May beauty quickening in beauty
Bring wisdom's fragrance to the mind
To grace your thought and work and love:
Seek a fine house, wise friends and fame.

In my rough youth I could not think
But garland you the queen of day
With desire's rhetoric:
You grace the evening of my dreams.

1955

LOVE OVERGROWS A ROCK

Only the foreground's green;
Waves break the middle distance,
And to horizon the Atlantic's spread
Bright, blue and empty as the sky;
My eyot jails the heart,
And every dream is drowned in the shore water.

Too narrow room pressed down
My years to stunted scrub,
Blunted my sister's beauty
And my friend's grave force,
Our tribe's renewing faith and pride:
Love overgrows a rock as blood outbreeds it.

We take banana boats
Tourist, stowaway,
Our luck in hand, calypsos in the heart:
We turn Columbus' blunder back
From sun to snow, to bitter cities;
We explore the hostile and exploding zones.

The drunken hawk's blood of
The poet streams through climates of the mind
Seeking a word's integrity
A human truth. So, from my private hillock
In Atlantic I join cry:
Come, seine the archipelago;
Disdain the sea; gather the islands' hills
Into the blue horizons of our love.

1957

I AM THE ARCHIPELAGO

I am the archipelago hope
Would mould into dominion; each hot green island
Buffeted, broken by the press of tides
And all the tales come mocking me
Out of the slave plantations where I grubbed
Yam and cane; where heat and hate sprawled
Among the cane – my sister sired without
Love or law. In that gross bed was bred
The third estate of colour. And now
My language, history and my names are dead
And buried with my tribal soul. And now
I drown in the groundswell of poverty
No love will quell. I am the shanty town,
Banana, sugarcane and cotton man;
Economies are soldered with my sweat
Here, everywhere; in hate's dominion;
In Congo, Kenya, in free, unfree America.

I herd in my divided skin
Under a monomaniac sullen sun
Disnomia deep in artery and marrow.
I burn the tropic texture from my hair;
Marry the mongrel woman or the white;
Let my black spinster sisters tend the church,
Earn meagre wages, mate illegally,
Breed secret bastards, murder them in womb;
Their fate is written in unwritten law,
The vogue of colour hardened into custom
In the tradition of the slave plantation.
The cock, the totem of his craft, his luck,
The obeahman infects me to my heart
Although I wear my Jesus on my breast
And burn a holy candle for my saint.
I am a shaker and a shouter and a myal man;
My voodoo passion swings sweet chariots low.

My manhood died on the imperial wheels
That bound and ground too many generations;
From pain and terror and ignominy
I cower in the island of my skin,
The hot unhappy jungle of my spirit
Broken by my haunting foe my fear,
The jackal after centuries of subjection.
But now the intellect must outrun time
Out of my lost, through all man's future years,
Challenging Atalanta for my life,
To die or live a man in history,
My totem also on the human earth.
O drummers, fall to silence in my blood
You thrum against the moon; break up the rhetoric
Of these poems I must speak. O seas,
O Trades, drive wrath from destinations.

1957

FUGUE FOR FEDERATION

Only the bald scholar and dusty
Archivist remember him for
Jew or Gentile, Spaniard
Or Portuguese; he's sailed
Through breed and bounds and creed;
He joins two worlds, two ages;
Atlantic is his tombstone;
Time and twenty nations his testators.

Look, my black fingers pencil
His memory on an islet
He sailed by, a mere rock
He disdained. Frey Bartolomo
Fetched me from the Congo
Since the Arawak, soft and green
As lilies, and the Carib wild
As "latcho" would not, could not
Yoke, lift, dig, endure,
Nor suck sweet gold from ground
In the tall and succulent cane.

Lord, all the West Atlantic
Seaboard's seethed and suffered
Since his caravels. Hell
Followed him with sword, sweat, lust;
Legions of generations
Still cry hate, disdain Toussaint,
Black semblance of a man.
The Slave Trade's buried
But its eternal tares of scorn
Breed in our barren soul,
Batten on the black, despised blood.

Time rimes and runs and ruins.
The tapestry she stitches
Rots, renews, extends
Our histories from Colon.
What sailed he seeking? Did he
Discover it upon this windy
Tide-knocked shoal of islands?
In droughts, rains, hurricanes?
Did the gross sun bawl lying
Rhetorics to greedy huntsmen
Of a golden myth?

Twenty-one republics
Seek sovereignties of Freedom.
Poem and peasant wear the crown
El Rey Fernando wore
When Colon sailed.
Nations and islands, angry
Or lazing under flaming sun, swear
Harshly or dream languidly
Of good and gold-faced Demos
Coming careless as breeding,
Or bright and imminent as dawn.

And on this archipelago he misnamed,
Thinking he'd turned the corner
Of the earth – oh but the earth
Much vaster than he dreamed it
Now's shrunk much smaller than he saw it –
On the bitter sugar Indies,
The principalities of slaves,
Men's ideals advance, leap
Over seas, league islands
Small as his caravels
Named for his known saints.

So now they sail, set sail
To destinations of the heart's desire.
His courage is their compass.
Their hope bowls past Sargasso
Farther than his, past that
First landfall on his isle of hills
Where now his legendary ashes sleep.
Through storms and doldrums
Grow, go forward islands.

1958

CORN

Stiff-boned, knotted men
Hoe in their growing corn,
Patient, stubborn as their cattle,
Wearing out the changing weathers,
Wearing time in generations
Continuing on the earth like grain
Through cycles of their tended grain.

There is a mystery that grows
Between them and the corn that grows,
Between the sower and the seed
And earth that multiplies the seed,
The elemental trinity.
There is a blind faith in their blood
That turns in our bi-seasonal earth
Like the wood-sap and wind and rain.

II

This earth heart-trodden and heart-hoed
Blessed the peasant boy's bare feet,
This simple culture nurtured him.
This natural love.
And wandering Ulysses is drawn
By the tether of his blood
Back to the corn-womb of his folk
Where his father's bones are rock,
Where he ate the soft green grain.
The golden marrow of the earth
With which she tamed the ravening blood
Of man the tiger from the wood.

III

Look on the sower and the seed
That thrives between the rock and rain:
The sower's life, flung from his hand,
Dead to the earth, resurrected to the wind,
Blooms its mystery under heaven,
Bears the living lovely bread,
The body and the blood of life.
The seed, the saviour of mankind,
The corn made flesh, the flesh breathes word,
Dream and wisdom, faith and love,
Beauty binding God and man.

1958

SHE NEVER DIES

Old chroniclers and poets tell
That she wrecked kings and kingdoms,
That the gods lusted,
Lost godhead in her loins;
Yet none have loved her more
Than kings and priests and poets.

Pere Abelard, I remember you
Unmanned for your white moon.
You teach out of your tomb
That two loves tear the heart.
I know you, Shelley, and you, Byron,
You two poets, you fornicators,
You lovers and abductors of women.
And I think about you, Keats,
Dying and staring on one silly woman
As I at my full moon
More dark and passionate
Than Solomon's.

The living man must love.
He turns his cycle,
His eyes intently on his satellite.
Tristan and Antony were blinded,
And Homer saw her burning Ilium.
He sang, and every poet sings
Because her image maddens every heart,
Although the best and worst of her's
In a cloud, mysterious as a dream.
Find the dream's meaning
Find why she never ages, never dies,
Why young men dote on her
Who mocks old lechers' impotence
When they can no more rouse
Her young concupiscence.

1959

FOR A.A. CIPRIANI

And may the poet speak his epitaph
Who was so far removed from poetry
Yet was such a poet of humanity
His heart frenzied into anger, rhetoric and action
Each time he felt the people suffer wrong?

I saw him only once; I was a boy;
But I remember a squat tan man in khaki
Speaking on my playground – his speech so strange
To innocence; I recorded nothing but his image,
And have no phrase or fancy of his I may praise.

But I heard of him after from folk who loved him.
From books, from ranting politicians
Who rattle his desires like drums,
And I think he's as indestructible as legend,
As a martyr's funeral pyre,
And his bones are cool in their tomb of history
As Lincoln's or El Libertador's.

Genius has many names and many faces,
Is born of the hundred human races.
Come out of dangerous, ambiguous Europe,
His catholic love embraced barefoot Africa,
Indentured India, China and Syria.
He preached race, caste and colour meaningless
Across the parks and squalid districts of his city.

Let him reign in bronze or what they've cast him
Like or unlike him, in the city that loves him.
If he's a colour of clay it will content him.
His anxious kindly eyes regard us,
And his modest attitude reminds of his hope,
Our hope; of his gift, the rare gift, the love of man,
He spent himself with a saint's humility.

1959

143

NOTES FOR A NEW POEM

My barren pear tree keeps her leaves
And seems as prim and passionless
As spinsters, class professional,
Trotting into offices.

My fruitful pear tree's shed her leaves
But bears a pitiful poor score
Of ping-pong-ballish sort of fruit
Blistered by the burning weather.

Mistletoe's leeched to her.
Why do the fruitful suffer much?
The fertile womb, the fertile mind?
Why do Gauguin and Jesus weep?

Well, you're stationed south of Cancer,
Your chip is on Equator's shoulder,
Never watch your native sun
Burning naked every sky.

The hills are gone tobacco brown,
The poinciana's lost her leaves,
The cedar and the tamarind,
Crops are slaughtered in the fields;

As if a splinter from the sun,
Shot, a rocket to the earth,
Burns the shark-shaped island up
With an unconsuming fire.

You don't miss water till the tap spits air.
Rainmaker, make the farmer's rain,
Conjurer, shoot the cumuli,
O priest, persuade whatever god.

First thunder's like a dinosaur
Or Pharaoh's broken chariot wheels,
Or Hercules hauling a mill head
Out of pretty Maia's way.

A black and snailly cloud has veiled
The sun's harsh equatorial stare;
Lightning rips it and is gone.
Thunder crushes in the roof.

The rain sits black upon the sea,
Streams white from hillsides into plains,
The air's turned cool as feather drawn
Lightly on my hirsute hand.

Bulb and root and seed will sprout,
Insects leave their nestling holes,
Hidden cocooned eggs will hatch,
A myriad tiny lives comes out.

Plant corn and bean and melon now,
Rice fields will lie drowned as reefs,
Caroni, sleeping in her mud
Will wake and break out of her banks,

And, hauling mud ajoupas down,
Drown luckless chicken, dog and cat,
Make flotsam of the furniture
And poor canoes of coconuts.

Coats and umbrellas come out.
The lower city streets will flood,
The streaming traffic wheels will splash
Angry pedestrians at the legs.

Cricketers will huddle in
And glumly watch the black clouds gush,
While farmers measure gleefully
Every shower inch by inch.

This is the season the ducks like,
But there are those who never mind
A weather, wet or dry, — men such as I;
Dead at a sedentary trade.

1960

THE PICTURE

I would I were Rembrandt, had all that light,
My art his art, my paper for his canvas,
And see her so, to hold ever so,
A moment laughing in the running moment.

The wind turns gently through her rust-brown hair
And channels in her hollow cheek; her eyes
Alive with pleasure that her red mouth laughs;
A gesture like a phrase, a chord, a curve.

I would take care to show her in the world
That scorns and envies and outlaws her worth,
The freedom she must live, the gaiety she is,
The whole earth's love and pity she possesses.

I should take care to name the picture "Harlot",
Lest those who come, not knowing, but enraptured
By the wild beauty and the goddess gesture
Should say she was the duchess of my heart.

It would not be the first time nor the last
The truth were wronged nor the lie hidden in
The line or colour; the man must love the model,
Or the work comes stillborn from the soul.

Light rises in the mind: it filled Rembrandt's
And warmed him till he died. All that he looked at
Lives; all that he made burns like the sun:
Time cannot blind the vision of his spirit.

Time cannot burn the lovely legends down;
Their golden flame warms history's sodden heart.
Why, all that love and pity had Isolde,
And such beauty had the Magdalen.

1960

THE OLD WOMAN

As grey as time,
As wrinkled as faith,
Alone in her cottage
The twice-widowed woman
Stoops through her rooms
Dragging her old slippers
On her dusty floors.

What does she dream?
What tender ghosts
Revisit her bed?
Does she turn at a memory
As once to a touch,
As once she turned dreaming
Of puissant love,
Now her dry boughs no more
Tremble to Trades of desire?

O pitiless God
Who never removes
The cup of our shames,
Who sets old teeth on edge
With the old sour sins,
Who on the screen of the mind
Projects the harsh film
Of despicable days
Till we weep repentance
Self scorn and self pity,
Physic her lightly.

O pitiless time,
You never advise
The riot of spring
Nor the hot summer's lust

Of winter or drought;
You never warn mouths
That quiver and kiss
Of curses and wrinkles.
Oh, whether we tell,
Profane or sacred,
The beads of our days
You bring us remorse.
The unloved woman
Weeps the spurned womb,
The mother of Christ
Moans at her cross,
Bitter Aphrodite
Curses her ruin.

O pitiless world!
No one remembers her
In her coffin of age;
Not the tranced lovers,
Not the rollicking dancers.
Not the proud and the lovely.
Oh, she sits lonely,
Wistfully watching
Sky, cloud and landscape,
Hearing the knell of the sea
Tolling her on.
In her dusty rooms
She makes friends with the dust.

1960

HE JUGGLES IMAGES

He sees with blurred and dying eyes,
Without regret, without remorse,
With irony his own demise.
He juggles images of death,
Sees disease sneaking into bone
Till the worms come,
And bone stripped bare
Lies white and quiet in a fold
Of sombre, unbreathing mould,
Or drowned and sucked under the sea,
Down to the never-never tide,
Is swayed among the dark sea stones
And stroked by soft sea anemones.

But who may dream all day of death?
Old lascivious eyes still watch
Two flattered streams of blood become
In their utter moment one.
Habit's husbandry abed,
Feline lovers on the grass –
Lust makes all the miracles;
For if concupiscence decays
Earth shall shudder in her ways
And every conjured god shall die.
The carnal eye's delighted in
The frenzy of original sin,
Grins as the seed in its wet sack
Hollows the prim virgin's back.

After its nurture in the womb,
On the breast and in the home,
That long nurture in the schools,
Recovering in the present tense
History's experience,

The mind makes reconnaissance
In the insane public dance.
Private experience,
The thin thread of a thousand strands —
How easy seems the bourgeois way!
Pray for those whose bitter fate
Falls into a most intricate,
Delicate, deluding dream;
Pray for makers and wreckers of dreams,
Wearers and weavers of robes without seams.

The light rises, the light dies.
Old grumbly gaffer, wrinkle-eyes,
Old hag stumbling with a stick
Were once concupiscent and quick.
In fifty years does death begin
To branch its cancer under skin.
Even the tough bourgeois goes,
Even iron-clad politicos —
Poor love sheds petals like the rose.
Do we rocket to the sun
Or ride a broomstick to the moon?
Pythagoras or Christ, tell me,
Show the point upon the circle,
The meaning of the miracle.

1961

THE CURSE OF HER BEAUTY

Wind-harried, tough
And twisted trees,
Burnt black by bitter
Sea spray flying
From the barrier rock;
That clay-brown woman
Slim as saplings,
Old as ocean,
Young as mornings.

O poet, O fool
That saw beauty walk
On the wind and the sea
To him on the rock!
No woman so lovely,
No kisses so sweet.
Love tinted that shore;
He thought her a goddess
Till he knew her a whore.

The corpse of his love,
A fragment of heart-wreck
Still knocks on those rocks.
Legend, deceiving as she is,
Has fixed her in the frame
Of the siren coast,
The wind-harried day,
The stained, tortured trees
Where the curse of her beauty
Branded his heart.

1961

MOTHER AND SON

Born to her middle years
He never saw her beauty's bloom
But he resurrects her youth,
Rebuilds her aged skin and bone,
Reburnishes it with purest love.

Her son saw her tough as scrub,
Stone-strong yet pliant as her clay,
Hoeing in the sloping fields,
Building up potato banks,
Nurturing the peasant earth.

Her sturdy arms in brown corn dough
She thumped and baked in plantain leaves
In the dirt oven in the dooryard –
Sweet corn bread is in his blood
Like peasant patois on his tongue.

Her humble rectitude was a rock
Outcropping of the stubborn land;
She sowed him barefoot like a tree
That he should eat the patient clay,
The solemn courage of the stone.

All her learning from one book,
She taught him time and tears began
In that sweet dream her death re-enters.
Hearing her speak the speech of prophets,
Tell memoried psalm and miracle

He entered a dry womb of words,
A Merlin's maze he cannot leave,
That gives salt grief to her old age.
He sees her stubborn dying eyes
Weep for him crossed upon his rhyme.

1961

153

THE WORLD OF ISLANDS

Watch from a journey close to cloud
A shoal of sea-beleaguered lands,
Siblings of the glaring sun
Grin their dolphin teeth at heaven.

A difficult country to inherit:
Guilt is humid in the glittering air;
Grafted at every branch the human wood
Blooms a bewildering scent, fruits bittersweet;
Indigenous blood still stains the grass;
Dragon's teeth still rattle under root,
And under stone the cold snake's coiled asleep,
Rapt in its murderous dream.

Those whom bondage bit to bone,
Who early learnt to sieve black grief
Through hardihood and song and prayer,
Repaint the tragic mask.
The shattered man sewn in the rock
Arises smiling like the surf,
Reaching to kiss each wind,
Groping to clouds for love.

The drummer with his father's knuckles
Knocks the torrid drum of the sun;
The dancer shakes her castanet the moon
To the loud rhyme of love, calling:
Come, come I am the phoenix Eve,
The mingled wine of the world's grapes;
I am the supple rhythm of the seas;
I recreate the world on islands.

1962

BLUES FOR UNCLE TOM

(Written for Martin Luther King on the occasion of his death)

now is the time
to mourn, not that he died,
but that they insulted us with his death
slew him in scorn of the race
in a public place in a harsh season.
slave blood groaning at their root,
his dripping blood this season's fruit,
his southern trees moan out the moses blues,
those tragic threnodies of tribes in trauma.
"by the waters of babylon…"
"tell ole pharaoh…"
yeah lord…
tears gleam in the sun's eye
and the moon's sigh draws earth's breath in pain.

we will not be satisfied
with the vine of his rhetoric
nor to name him in his cool idiom
christ, lincoln, kennedy
nor any coon preceding him on the lynching tree
till shiloh come,
till time or god or fate we care not which
or the white man our nemesis enfranchises us.
o man, they nailed him to his death,
to silence and to history –
god judged his prayers too loud, discomfiting heaven,
discomfiting those nordic lands
where black is a negation,
death, devil's masses, witches,
riding abroad horrendous sabbaths,
pogrommed to drowning pools and funeral pyres;
black their ancestral fear of forest wombs,
fen waters and wolf-howling winter nights,

black lustings for poor scapegoats for this guilt,
into this maddening plague of hate for our black skins.

"i have a dream," he cried, "i have a dream",
his rhetoric drumming doors of immortality,
demanding that his bloodied head
stand a stalagmite in time.
but we have grieved past statues,
we have prayed too long for deliverance,
we are weary of servitude;
our pride's an ancient scarecrow
tattered by raw weathers, is poor old
uncle tom, poor featherhead
stretched dead on hope's hard bed.
we come from caves of history
into these ghettos that garrotte our dreams
and burn love's hope back to its stump of stone.

hurricanes howl in canyons,
between our antipodal skins,
deep-down bestial chasms of untime, unplace,
unhistory, frog-spawning passions,
and the gods gaze in them and yawn wearily
and spit on the skin of pride
and arrogance and gold.
Ogun and Javeh!
slaver after slaver stank atlantic
each swaying mass plunging the penis of scorn
through the vagina of fear to breed
this age of hate, to spawn these martyrdoms
whose actors sweat their barren seeds of blood
that know no resurrection, lord,
no easter morning for our mourning.

1972

AT GUARACARA PARK

the bronze god running;
beauty hurtling through the web of air,
motion fusing time and space
exploding our applauses...

speed was survival there in the green heat
where the lithe hero dashed
from the leopard's leap,
fled to cover from the feral fang
or ran the antelope across the plains.

and speed and stamina were the warrior's pride
where impis of assegais and swords and shields
tore tigerish through the brush and raided
and bounced back upon the kraals
panting from wounds and weariness,
brandishing the trophies of their cradling war.

The slave ships could not break our bones
nor strip our tendons, nor the long slaving
years narrow our arteries nor disease
our lungs nor shrivel up our hearts,
but left love thundering to this running man.

not fame's wreath crowns him
but Ogun's aura now; that blaze of flame
that savaged history back beyond our memories
our dreams and searchings.
the blood of the fierce gods we lost,
the pantheon of the kraals made him immortal
or he would have been a scarecrow in the canes.

1970

CITY CENTRE '70

at city centre here,
in this green square
the stone men closed,
the trees stand witness
that men do not die
but grow in dreams of generations
bitter and beautiful as cedar leaves,

by flooding tides of wrath and beauty
in the harsh comedy of history,
that love distils like the trees' sap
from the disease of tyranny
and shame's corruption
that shut up the square.

the trees condescend that we,
wayfarers in the traffic
and in time, should see them
with eyes cold to their beauty
statued living in eternity
here where we've jailed them in the square,
forlorn as exile on the Boca rock.

laurels crown
their great immobile marathons
their green turns brown
and brownness, the earth's colour,
falls to earth where the great
cycle reaffirms itself,
rejoins eternity and greens again.

we cannot stand and wait:
our turbulence burst like bombs
and guns under the patient trees,
roared from our streets and homes.
poor Abel tunes his threnodies, his blues;
Cain's conscience smokes:
Guilt sears his arteries like flame.

1970, 1972

CARIBBEAN CALYPSO

I

Roads were rougher in their island kingdom
When Shakespeare cut and chiselled at his verse
And Marlowe, martyred in a brawling tavern,
Was made immortal on the kiss of death,
His bright blood streaming in the firmament...

The kingdom was the royal woman's fief,
The poignard was sharp private enterprise
And the long sword a prized inheritance;
Heroes dreamed great Viking voyages
Westward Ho! Sails through Colon's horizons
And, ah well, Drake's still at Nombre Dios.

John Hawkins pounced upon a continent,
Kidnapped the innocents in paradise
Middle-passaged for the Spanish Indies
Telling his psalms to Trades; bartered, sold me
For indigo, molasses, cotton, spice
And such sort of savoury merchandise.

II

Those whom bondage bit to bone,
Who early learnt to sieve grief's stones
Through hardihood and prayer and song
Repaint the tragic mask;
Buried living in the clay,
Resurrected to the sun
They yearn to kiss the clouds,
To fondle the moon's drum
And thrum the Trades' guitars.

They chorus calypsos –
Lusty flagella
For dancers' bawdy hips –
But platonic time instructs
The ignorant to wrest
Wisdom art and song
From the loins of joy and grief.

III

A net was wrought to seine
Antilles to our hope,
Archipelago to state,
Where once our nigger hate
Cursed the bitter cane,
The isles it could not flee
And the imprisoning sea.
New seasons kissed plantations,
Droughts conceived and bloomed,
Ratoons of canes and slaves
Swore sweet blood brotherhood
And called from parishes
To sea-bound parishes
In the mid-century swim.
But asses brayed
And the brittle dream shattered
To shards of cays and shoals
That pricked our hearts to tears.

IV

The drummer and the drum
Sprung of the ancient womb
Crouch at the tree's root
And are her flower and fruit;
A voice and a guitar
Serenade a star.

The hoe-man and his sweat
Knead immortal corn
Into mortal bread
To the fierce rime of need;
Hands of reapers pluck
Rum from a ripe stalk.

Prisoners of history
Our skin and circumstance
We have small room to dance;
A thin shard of land
Defiant of the sea
Defines our destiny.

V

Water is no mirage where there is always water;
Dwellers by blue-green bays, on hilltops over oceans
Know dreams walk easily as sandalled Christ
On seas blue as his gospel truth
Pilgrim to ancestral sources
To find home nowhere from these summery islands,
Nowhere beyond the tide marks on their creeks;
For, on each wave of his far voyages,
Even in Circe's arms,
Odysseus yearns for the sun-drenched,
Wind-blistered, rain-sweetened kingdom
Where he walked barefoot in baronies of cane
And fiefs of corn and yams
In the sound of private seas...
In laboratories of islands, the sun
Compounds chemicals of cultures, colours, tongues
Strange everywhere but in their hothouse homes.

And here the songsmith tunes
The stiff Shakespearean rime,
To the lilt of Cancer's seas.
Listen, the lyric drum
Swings laughter, love and grief
Through one melodic line.

1970

BALLAD FOR TUBAL BUTLER

When I met him face to face
he had become a poor buffoon,
a decrepit toothless hound
whining at his private fleas.
Yet, proud and raging in his prime,
his anger set a blazing torch
to centuries rotten with our shames
and singed the old slave tapestry.

Corporal King died roaring in
a bonfire of the season's sins;
a British officer named Powers
was executed by the mob
whose rage and hatred, fear and need,
roused to desperate bloody deeds,
flayed fat folly to awareness
and thrust politics a theme.
Then every liar in the land,
village lout and city snip,
every rogue turned orator;
not one hibiscus blazed unseen.

Now the heroic man grown old
eats the pap of the mad Lear.
I've heard him rant and seen him mocked
because history's ceaseless flood
has left him on a muddy shoal,
sometimes baying at the wind,
sometimes howling, a mad dog,
at the current in its course.

1972

164

ELEGY FOR N. MANLEY

Lodge him securely,
set him a monument
against seismic movements
of minds and mountains.
Our climate's harsh to death
that bloats and rots
in the engendering sun;
worms are quick to our oblivion.

The rotten tapestry
of mastery and slavery
was his swaddling cloth;
the hoe of hope
and the pronged pitchfork
of politics were his hand tools
to tear slave middens down,
to plough them deep into Jamaica soil
and seed it new with freedoms.

In his long labourings,
anguished to the bone,
he sweated under history's
fierce sun of wrath
until he fell face down
in the dross of slums
and wretched stony fields
snarling with hatreds;
his sighs were sounds of tired
ocean rollers dying in our bays,
mists of his Blue Mountains
snowed his head.

In his decrepitude
all his hope, work, faith
lay waste like dead leaves in a drought;
the barefoot black still languished,
still despised, and his brown caste,
drunk on the rum of arrogance,
self-seeking and contempt,
stood monstrous in the land.
He knew all he had done
was to proffer his once handsome face
for this fine effigy for fools.
He turned his broken spirit to the night.

1972

PIARCO

Whole villages come
cliqued, cawing like poggoes
round one they're posting
into alien seasons,
civilisations that broke
and twined us round their will.
Each brings him gifts
a handclasp or a kiss,
jewels even, of tears,
to ease the boy's umbilical
severing from the clan,
yet moor him by love's hope
in the green pool of home.

They suffered centuries
of time's distilling
of the peasant blood,
of sighs from penury and pain
in their Homeric grappling
with the earth to gain this day,
this font through which the son
who rode the bison to the pond,
split cacao pods, cut canes,
threshed rice, reaped peas in season
shall name them to the world.
Their eyes are gleaming
with new years of dreams.

She waddles, wheels,
exhales a dragon breath
blasting the waving gallery,
children laugh and women scamper off

She's come from Bogota;
and those there – read their names –
from Buenos Aires, Rio, Santiago:
they flew up the long Antarctica – touching
America del Sud
to rest like migrant birds
on our sea rock
at the equatorial hinge
of the American mass.

One lifts and noses
north for New York,
Toronto, Montreal;
then she'll bear east
across Atlantic on to London;
there, all Europe's cities
are a choice of journeys –
Paris, Berlin, Rome –
and what is beyond is dreams.

Islands cage us
and we long to leave them;
the cities scorn us
and we long to love them.
Bite the earth's orange
And her pips are bitter.

1972

POEM

Dying, the serpent's
writhing in its coils
tombing itself
in fold on fold
of its cold quivering flesh;
awful the death throes.

Who struck the coup de grace?
No one, no one.
The thing undid itself.
Threshing in torments
of guilt, of fear, of folly,
its spine slipped discs;
Anguished, it wrings its life
from the necrotic rope.

Well, let it die.
Who grieves a serpent's death?
No one, no one.
It ruined paradise
despoiled our virgin innocence
and will devour
each pure Utopia
we may dream.

1972

POEM FOR THIS DAY

giddy upon repelling slopes,
crawling like maggots into swamps,
clapboard and tin, sad prey for rains,
high winds rattling their hides like leaves,
the poor slums fester in the heart,
the shantytowns, the squatters' tenements;
indigence sweats these vermin-peopled huts.

regard these market towns and mouldering
villages we find on motoring roads
as if astonished of their presences
carved out of forests, canefields,
cocoa, coconut and coffee groves;
not even names to us as we cruise by
in shades of opulence,
in varying degrees of cool contempt
sheltered from their sun of poverty,
sneering at their gnarled and barefoot drought.

you'd think the state too stern for mercies
or the earth's blood, bitter as aloes,
is too bitter to suckle these poor folk;
that charity's atrophied in the heart
too sterile for love's silken roots.

village labour sweats among its trees
on the tough soil of hope
where men grow bovine in their bovine round
of work, feed, sleep and blind begetting
which they can break only if they abandon home

to prodigal in the sour slum
with those who've failed their hope
like writers their weak talents;
failed, failed lives
failed spirit and failed love.
and there it's all amen, amen,
save for the politician's cloven tongue,
his teeth rotting with his foul deceits,
handouts and handcuffs,
the circus guarded with tear gas and guns.
all that goes free are rats and roaches;
all left of liberty is abuse of power;
all left to live is drunkenness and lust
and mania for the bestial carnival.

1972

HARD DROUGHT

We marched in Butler's
barefoot mad battalions
in a damned time
on the slave world's slipping edge;
our arms were rhetoric
and they shot us down
and scattered us to the Trade Winds;
we shook the pillars of the place and wept.

Williams called us
and we thought we'd won;
we set him on the golden stool,
gave him kingdom upon kingdom
of the heart; our pride and love
ringed him with janizaries.

Confusion fell upon us
as we learned on the years' marches
that he was not ours but history's ruin,
his homing instinct's back to barracoons
and slave plantations.
Damballa laughed
Jehovah sneered
They sent no Moses season
no one of Toussaint's valour
nor Joshua's genius for the craft of war.

We were a mob;
our barricades fell down on our own braying
Jackals have whinnied in the lion's lair.
A cruel cunning lodged that *grappe*
of fools where Butler lodged
a generation gone; their rank piss
fouled the old man's tattered sheets.

This veteran of griefs, betrayals, shames
snarls in the ancestral void
where the Middle Passage flung us
on our knees. And in my one whole ear
I hear the moles purr in the silent dark
among the stones... these wretched murmurations...

Don't mock me about dreams
I am too old.
Don't sneer of prophecies
count me among the numberless dead
this grisly century.
I've eaten so much history that I belch
boloms of years to come.
Drunk each day's carnival
I leer and squint at time telescoped
In Jesus' spear-cleft side.
We shall not build
a kingdom of this world that is not ours

Station by station throughout history
the ground is bloody; the hero's face
stamped on the woman's napkin's masked in blood.

1973

VERSE IN AUGUST

For Frank Collymore

knock drum
draw bow
on fiddle strings
let rhythm jump
    and catgut screech
let all time jig
a kalinda and reel
these august freedom days
let dead bones rise
and dance their own bongos

who'll dance my death farewell?
who'll trample me a rhythm on my grave?
            "bongo macedonia
            viniway viniway bongo"
not my tall sons
they have not seen nor heard
that macabre rime of death
and if they did
    i could not answer their disdain
they have inherited another season
    in this uprooted suburb
    of folk from villages and slums
where dusks brood secret hatreds
    and faces are tight shut
from love and friendship.

my life began among kind folk
    whose barefoot indigence was whole
    as rocks and springs, whose love
    nourished life's roots

whose labour was
a cutlass hoe and spade
in plots of corn and yams.
i knew some legendary men
   i know them still
they're fast in file on film
   a thought reanimates them
whom only my death will bury
for they're mine, they're mine
until my body lays me down.

i knew that cruel cunning man
   old pa ben gordon grumbling in his beard
   mumbling evil at the world
threatening jumbie obeah
   and harder vengeances
on those humbugging him
   the world humbugged him.
thumping his stick on the ground
railing at me always railing
   pouring all molten hell into my bones
   at first i feared and then i hated him.
my mother said the devil fathered him
   she was his kin
   as real as life
these 50 years he's mummied in me
his stick his grey beard
and his guile and grumbling.

i saw br'angas once
   kneel under killing blows
his poui warding death
     "mumma, mumma,
      you son in de grave arready

       he down in de grave arready"
he rose from that
his fierce eyes bleeding vengeance
his squat thick body leaping
   the stick flailing,
the drums choked on a note
   and his foes fled.

rum drums and singing men
   gambash in the gayelle
   carray! ah bois garcon!
   ah ah! ah ah!
      "*hooray hooray cutoutah*
      how much hero you kill in arima?"
bloodshed on freedom day
rum drums and broken heads.
ah august kalindas!
all that long ended
but i have it still
   a bright splash on the mind.

i knew men pushing out to sea
at dusk in bare canoes
wave skimming wooden shells
i watched the steady rhythm of their oars
diminishing on the sea scape
till darkness took them
a-morning they returned
naked as fish,
wet as the dripping sea
summoning us with conches
and slow haul up of boats out of the tide.

hot days in glittering bays
white-waved fawn-sanded and
    green-fringed with palm and sea grape trees
the girls loved under the sea grape trees
    all that pure loving for the loving's sake
    the animal ecstasy of the ignorant blood.
The days stand up to bless me
    as i die
bedded on my dying century
dreaming the century's youth
    in a good place that's gone
    among the folk i loved
while my own death
howls from a mangy dog
haunting these barren streets.

what's all my witness for?
why do i wear the poor folk and the years?
eh brother what's the score?
is the game won or lost?
will i know now
at the breaking bitter last?
do old men know?

1973

UNPUBLISHED POEMS
A SELECTION
1945-1974

GIRL, GODDESS, BITCH

In shade I contemplate
your sunspot on my hand;
Your shadow trails me
in the sun, and in the dark
those scornful eyes,
that mocking mouth
gleam like a cluster of stars –
Girl, goddess, bitch,
I've lived and died
between your loins;
and loved and hated you
from boyhood, and still
My manhood's poled upon your will.

c.1945-50

GIRL

Do not be hurt or angry
that I laugh; I do not wound
you, do not wound yourself;
wear my laughter
for a cloak
to shield you from a rain of harms.

I think that if I touched
your hair's cool curls, the tides
would rise, lightnings, hurricanes
and thunders strike;
and if you had
nine lives all would be lost.

1954

SONG

Buy her wine and roses,
gladden her laughter,
tell her she's legend
like Leda's daughter,
a boldly made beauty
aching the eye, Isis, Astarte.

But never ask her
of hearts that keep honour,
puritan modes,
ethics and codes.
Cords that should bind her
to one bed
crumble in
her passionate blood.

To the body only
that ripe beauty,
golden as honey
hum your canzone.

The hunter's cry and shriek
of the hunted shatter the scapes;
starved children bloat remorselessly
to death that drinks their tragedy
of folly as it ate Christ's flesh;
evil is a quicksand lurking
for innocence as guilt,
for love as loneliness
subtle in Cancer as in Arctic.
Anguish blights the private mind;
computers plot the death of cities;
precise skilled gunners annihilate
a landscape and for that wasteland
tough battalions wrestle.
Yet the wind sighs, the sea laughs,
the fish swims in its cool;
only the eye, piercing the scale,
strikes blind to the real bone
with which fear's trembling hand
writes rhymes on a slate of sand.

c.1960

BETWEEN TWO LIVES
(extract)

Africa's a slavish bitch,
a trusting slut lascivious Europe raped;
in dreams I fondle her with love,
in sweating noons
I stare at her with hatred and contempt,
she's ecstasy and anguish in my guts.

Centuries on centuries of middle passages
laden with her siblings, slave ships sailed
south at Mossamedes, north far as Dakar,
spoked out on routes
to reach the long trans-ocean seaboard
north of New York
and beyond Buenos Aires southward to Antarctic.
Now midway on Columbus's green cays
Crusoe and Friday are marooned together
their love-hate coupling in sardonic cane
exhausting bitterness in fornications,
breeding mestizos.

Ah, we are castaways of many names –
creole, nigger, darkie, spade
and every island name. It all depends
on where we are, what tribes we trespass on.

. . . .

Where is the secret track,
the hidden hunter's path
through history's undergrowth and hate's
that we may crawl or swing simian
through what trees
through what long centuries
to come at last on islands in what seas
or soft plains between rivers

shadowed by mountains
that shall bring us rain
from our own gods again
transfiguring us to men?

THE DEAD ARE MANY LESS

The old hound feels his skeleton obtrude
And all his thought descants on death.
Libraries of elegies have rotted
Like old hides; mountains of mummy cloth
Piled thick as cumuli have not kept Pharaohs warm;
Boulders bolstering each death
Against the tempest of time's fires
Moulder in middens with Astarte's lust;
The dead are meaningless as stone.

"Three paths go to the well,
Three turnings to his end,
A man takes one;
The choice is in his stars," the old man said.
"Live unloved,
Apart from the caress of men and angels,
Upon your lonely pilgrimage
Silently re-entering eternal silence.
The beloved filters through the needle's eye,
In the hemlock of a lover's tears —
That one alone whose life joined yours.
But, rare as martyrdom
Or as the visitation of a saint,
Is death by drowning in the wave
The sluggish tide of human love."

He died as lonely as a wounded bird;
The earth has gorged his skeleton.
He shrinks in the museum of my mind
And sneers at the destruction of my life
That has made nothing
But shards and shingles of loose words
Sun, wind and rain have knocked about,
Sent scurrying like black leaves in drought

Into the limbo of this evil century.
The pity's in the jest that all my annelid generation
Crawls between the soil and stone bewildered for the light.

DRUNK ON RUM

I sit alone in a cafe
drinking rum and plain tap water
talking terms with Mr. Death,
feeling civilisation patter
past the window of my eye,
rattling the shutters of my heart –
dead generations stumbling by
upon the impulse of their sex,
the pulsing vigour of their blood
that heaps the dead upon the dead
season and dynasty
into the earth's eternity.

Had they built since Nineveh
mountain on mountain of men's bones,
the summit soaring past the sun
had burst the golden floors of heaven
and God's grace come pouring through
the hollow of each pelvic bone,
and on the ground had given birth
to the miraculous rose of love
as fragrant in each generation
and every common fool's been blest.

OLD DOGS

That shattered joy,
that old abandoned jug
from which the rum's run out...
for years she graced the harlotry
marketing her worsening wares
till her clientele fell off.

It broke her heart
when an old foul-mouthed lout
reported on her fleshiness:
"She is a log the sea washed in
from floating down the Amazon
onto the island of her bed."

An old roué,
a flea-ridden and scabietic hound
crouched in a dead wall's shade
heedless if the moon silvers its paws
or graces the Antipodes,
jesting at a long-dugged bitch.

Wonder gone, innocence spent,
Christmas passed to the desert days of Lent,
dead love, dead pity...
dust rising from a wasted land...
And one foolish fond old man,
mad at the heart for miracles,
sniffs back his young love's scented sheets,
dreams bloom on leafless dying trees.

ONLY THE DEAD

Within the sea's disdain
beneath the sun's contempt
knocked by the wind's mockery
we live, we mini-men on rocks
outside the mainstream of man's
Mississippi rolling through time
that is the thunder of all marching minds,
not the feet of legions
of lost lifeless generations
but those of Aristotle, Quattrocento,
philosophers, poets
and the blessed makers of mad music
streaming into the mysteries of the moon;
not yet for us those footpaths through the wood.

Islands are backwoods,
into which the tired wander
with cameras and weary eyes
to renew the wasted substance of their blood
in primitive vitality,
in the verity of sands and seas;
asylums yes,
from which all those minds, lit
by the volcanic sun, who, born to know
the anguish of God's love,
the loveliness of roses,
to dream of glories stored in the fierce blood
must stumble from those vegetable cays,
these Eden days of nothing into flame.

And so it goes;
the best bolt off
into the endless masquerade of exile,
desert these squalid dooryards

where men demeaned themselves with slavery
and their slaves grew vile with hatred

and their joint heirs scramble a giddy tightrope
to certain doom that's not enough to live for.
We are lost; history despoils us;
all the old follies griefs and wraths
hound us to leap like demented swine,
like the lost tragic tribes
over the precipice to the shrouding sea.
Only the dead preserve their sanity.

TALL IS NOT

Tall is not Tucuche nor teak
nor cedars: quit the dark timber,
turn your back on mountains;
they are inviolable as time,
are always rocks round which our
blood knocks its recurrent tides.

Stand clear to westward of decadent
Europe that taught us all that damn
romantic humbug of dwarfish man
before beanstalking nature; stand where
it's human; tall is a man a-tip-toe,
whirling his tribe's dreams, sparking
a rainbow halo round his head;
tall is a man who reaches other men
across the tribeyards of their griefs and hatreds.

Faith stands tall that fertilises
hope into the seeds of deed, enriches
the earth's mead of happiness,
outlawing pain, spreading love's
honey on the bread of days;
and any gift to human worth
is monumental as a mountain
and remains.

AT SANGRE GRANDE

"*Here the Negro, the Chinee,*
the white man, the Indian
walk together in hand
in this wonderland of calypso,
this wonderland of steelband"
        Calypso chorus by Lord Baker.

The jungle presses
we hold a clearing only,
like the late Arawak
that poor mushroom man,
peering at sneering skies.

No distance challenges
our myopic eye;
we hate, lust, fornicate,
cluster and vegetate
like the rain forest around us.

All night the Hindu drums
and chants his baroque East
communicating home,
shaming the creole man's
shabby masquerade.

Fo Chin, in sleeveless vest,
keeps shop, grinning his pidgin,
strumming his cash register,
his eyes slant to the score,
humming a dollar aria in his head.

Dr. Geneticist Lust
experiments with us
crisscrossing seed,
splitting each breed
to quaint improbable mutations.

But stocks hold true
guarding their pith;
Hindu and Muslim snarl, Chinese
and whites stand off – blacks
seethe and rage in contempt of themselves.

The sun's displeasure
glares on man and mosque;
the moon despises
these rank simian hatreds
of customs, skins and creeds;
the swamps stink with our shames.

c.1963

CARNIVAL

    asses bray, goats bleat,
    monkey's jabber their unintelligible
    language; parrots, macaws
    shatter the air, squawking inanities;
    turkeys gabble in drummed rhythms
    preening assumed plumage;
    the city's sweating in the gathering garbage.

We lost a continent, our rivers dried up;
legends died at our ancestral roots
where hardiest horsemen, spearsmen, bowmen
raged and impis sneered at death.
The clown's ascendant here: old wisdom's
tumbled from his rope of reason down on
our witless gaping faces –
the tribal face one leering Comus mask
sweating in the city's teeming garbage.

    bang tambourines,
    grapple with guitars and saxophones,
    rattle hysteria till the town
    yells bedlam; hovel, backyard
    and slum shriek in delirium,
    and the rum-drunk bacchanal
    of folly, fear, frustration, lust,
    malice and hatred roars in the streets
    of sweating obscenity and reeking garbage.

Choruses of bawdy calypsos
obscene as carrion crows
darken the sunlight with cacophonies
that desecrate all that harmony

the serpent's cunning taught us.
All art and grace and fine delight
is drowned in frenzy of the carnival
that steeps the city in lust, sweat and garbage.

1962-63

A NEW TIDE RUNNING

A new tide running over ancient rocks
you laugh on all my years till now I dream
my death reversed, that I grow young
while you grow up and see your noon of beauty
blaze on my returned maturity.

Undying never happened though; the myth
of miracles expired with man's faith
and innocence; I've lived too long already;
my future is a dark ghost of memory
through your years; a face that scenes, cares,
dreams crowd into twilight thoughts
of one who loved you for yourself alone
across the decades that divide our lives,
across experiences you can't surmise.

Grow cool and lovely; keep something
of you in the mists of mystery;
men love decorous and charming women
not totally exposed to scrutiny;
fools and mere statues, magnets to the worst,
pursuing worthlessness, sequined
with vanity, wreck dreams and kingdoms.

The world grows crowded and more vulgar;
minute by minute, more mad millions swarm;
everywhere the worst is popular;
Christ is shrinking from the multitudes;
it grows impossible to preserve
the soul's aloneness, not to be faceless
as a grain of sand nor anonymous as seed
in the vast city silos
not to be smothered in the stink of slums,
the lethal rage and grief of ghettos.

Be queenly in your thoughts, be generous
to folly and the poor, forgive the rich,
avoid fanatic men stalking in hatred
through their dragon dreams, scorn those
who blinded by their assumed brilliance
cannot appraise the starshine of your gifts.

Renewing generations of our youth
took us on golden transports to the moon
where Aphrodite of the flesh and blood
and bed and fertile juices of our sex,
more burnished in her image than pure gold,
reigned, reigned and reigned in many revered names.
But science has burnt up the mists of myths,
broke her fine images, flushed faerydom
down sewers; sweet Titania's dead;
love's dreams are shattered by machines
shuttling unimaginable miles.
And, if you ship there for your honeymoon,
think of the dead of earth, the ancient dust
of love's green sap that nurtured you;
grant me that memory for an epitaph.

1961-65 c

THE SUN GLARES

The sun glares lidless at these rocks
that blocked Columbus's course and killed
his hunt for landfalls of fine gold,
for India in her aromatic seas
after our sea sargassoed him
and fouled his keels of dreams.

He shipped damnations into every bay –
cargoes of Castillian louts,
lusts, saints and sicknesses.
Europe's bloody minded rogues,
sworn berserk to the sword,
squashed the potato tribes into the clay.

Soldiers and slave farmers notched their days
with slave girls' maidenheads,
castrated slave revolts,
dragged miscegenation,
rum, molasses and mad hate
across recurrent sugar seasons.

Clusters of drums whose folk bare feet
kicked time across the kraals
descant and still descant
on ancient mummied cadençes,
hounding live dancers to dead ecstasies,
rousing new waves to wander on old seas.

Caribbean today:
pickles of old bloods,
old cultures, certitudes
seethe in uncertain fermentation,
smarting our throats,
starting a stream of tears;

flotsam from China's floods,
the Indus delta and the Congo mud,

Astarte's tumult and the Saxon
snows meet mate and hate.
The sure prognosis is: "Men's guts will bleed
while islands stumble on their odysseys
now their slave-sugar Iliad is ended."

SENGHOR VISITING

Your presence is our past,
is all that we have died
since our dispersal,
all that has settled down
to lees in our folk mind,
dancers' and drummers' lore, languages
coffles, ships and passages.

Castaways, seaweed and flotsam
have small choice;
the ocean drinks
them back or runs them through
the coastal mangrove roots
to rot or barnacle; cast ashore
from slavers, sir, we fertilised
these islands, sweetening Europe's cups,
ripening tobacco blacker than our skins
with sweat and fear and hate,
hiding the drum between the loins,
hoarding its rhythms precious in the heart.

This flock of rocks, fleece
of the grand Columban legend,
shorn now of innocence, butchered
by churches, wars and politics,
and left for worthless sullen parishes…
Well, take this one, this wart
on South America's cheek, this enigma
that Spain took, France colonised
and Britain plundered and gave law
and language, then hauled in Asia's
siblings for survival,
as Bligh brought breadfruit from far happier islands…

You're farther off from Dakar
than you know; our history's ocean,
time, miscegenation, new worlds,
visions, hybrid vigours and new dreams
divide us from your monolith.
Minute by minute
and face by neighbour face skins change
as in a tapestry a woman weaves in rainbow hues;
mosques, temples, churches,
costumes, languages jostle in the mosaic
as if we kept carnival for the world
or a fair to which all nations came.

Yet if we talk a little
you may find something stronger
than a rotten thread stringing
old crumbling beads. The Trade Winds
lost their force since America swallowed
the industrial age, and our Caribbean,
in which imperial bubbles formed and burst,
receded to this quiet backwater
where tourists bask in the green sun
of legend. Once golden colonies of forts
and guns and slaves and canes
are knick-knacks now, and sugar's serfs,
their memories dim as dreams,
recross the ocean seeking their lost sources.

Old words the slave folk stored
for centuries in marrow bones
or molecules of the blood
with the drum's rhythms
come back to salt the tongue
across those distances you came
bringing your legend –
a chief in the old place,

a great one of the golden stools we lost;
so we salute you
through our kinship of the skin,
the sun complexion of your continent,
the badge of all who bear us brotherhood.

c.1964

THE PHARAOH'S EYE

Dead gods, dead ancestors, (egungun) hear us!
Leaderless, we turned to one
who shouted to us for kingship, telling us news
we greatly longed to hear – that after the dispersal,
after the slavery and degradation, after
obeisance at the white man's foot
we would ascend into man's majesty,
into the kingdom of all free men's hearts.
Our hopes applauded! God, how we applauded,
we carved a golden stool and set him on it
as we dreamed you old ones did in the lost kingdoms.
Thousands and thousands of hurrahs proclaimed him.

Applause subsides; not that
the hands grow weary or the hearts less warm,
but that the king's face or the god's assumes
the tragic or the comic mask or turns
to lust, folly, fear or forgery,
shaming or searing loves and loyalties.
Our hurt was that this king assumed no face we knew,
that he reneged, mocked tribal aspirations,
disavowed our dreams, kicked down our totem poles,
sneered at our myths and legends, put history
like his "gan-gan" in a cupboard, turned
his bland face to smile on hostile gods. Feeling
his instinct for betrayal, seeing his act,
our stunned hands stopped applauding.

Some say the fault is in ourselves, the dead rot
of four hundred years of serfdom settled like a mould,
a cancer in our spirit, has made us annelid
and him mere nothing, invalid in himself,
lacking directions save back into the mazes
of our wrath. With this we create

not kinship but a curse, and we have drunk, not wine,
but the sour vinegar our shames ferment
in centuries of serfdom. It maddened us.

Our rage exploded. Ogun, hear us.
He spilt our blood on streets where we acclaimed him.
He shot us down in the square of the carnival
where gay crowds bacchanalled.
Boys and old men were slain.
Our children screamed when the guns crashed
and the scared birds dashed off to safer places.

He reigns among the guns, but it is ended.
Our love that gave him life lies dead and stinks
in hatred. And this invalidates a king,
negates a man. Inscrutable Shango
of the unfailing phallus drenches him
in faeces; he reigns in odium; chronicled
in obloquy and contumely his name is ended.
Those whom he slew have passed into our pride,
Ascended to our legend and our myth;
the blood of martyrdom is deified.
And with my Eucharist, singing our *Missa
Negra,* man, we stumble on, still seeking freedom
in the Pharaoh's eye.

I SAY IT WAS THE WOMEN

(for all the tall upstanding sisters of the generation)

Hard poems bruise my mind
(you're one of them)
but I can't write them.
My slave age knees give way;
new tides of old ideas
shake my crumbling rock:
I fall asleep at the wrong moments
but I dream of your grave faces,
your dark earnest faces,
your daring voices hard in argument,
and in the dream I listen, I approve,
but in the bitter day I turn aside.
The long hard years confound me like a curse.

It's not been easy.
Since the Trade began
you perished; you gave birth in coffles
and slave ships; the children died;
they flung each stillborn foetus
to the sharks; you spawned on slave
plantations; some of your young
were you; some were a splinter tribe;
white was the seed but black the soil
and brown the issue of that raving age.
You worked and spawned and wept
and nurtured and endured
throughout the mad Slave Trade, the mad slave system.

A black cock's rhetoric,
but I say again
it's not been easy.
In the first freedom time

207

in wattle mud-straw huts
you cradled a new age with bare hands,
shaping civilisation
from cow dung and marl and sweat,
working provision grounds,
tending black cooking pots on stones
in dooryards while mosquitoes and flies
raged round from bush and filth
like Tartar horsemen.
I affirm it here,
I touched that generation and I know
that you gave suck and succour,
taught faith and love and hope
to your rock-clinging season
to lumbering men who else
had plunged into the precipice of chaos.
You raked the embers of the race
out of its ashes. Your breasts alone bridged eras.

In time, my time,
(don't doubt a poet's witness)
you cooked and washed and scrubbed,
planted and prayed and taught
in those harsh clapboard schools
that nurtured villages.
You fought too,
marching long barefoot marches
sweating, singing psalms
with the white captain and that Tubal Butler
killing the great beast that stood
between us and a brighter sun,
breaking hard barricades of history,
bursting an Empire's walls,
draining its fetid swamps.

Always some hide in terror
from the sweating seasons:
some turn to harlotry
and some disperse among the alien,
some under Jesu's robes;
and some go mad, staring in nightmare,
dreaming in the sun,
wailing like ghosts in alien cultures
from the broken ramparts of the race.
But still you turn and turn
to take the gown of honour,
the mud-stained shift, the purple of the race:
you kiss tradition, fate and circumstance.

Our gospel truth
is harder than we know it.
Written in the ink of blood,
molasses and spent sweat,
it reads:
Centuries of slavery
left the nigger naked,
stripped bare of human attributes
cropped back to the ape stock.
At one cold cutlass stroke religion went;
down fell another and the language went
and pride and names and cultures
all drained out like blood from mortal wounds –
Africa dismembered, disembowelled.

I die maintaining this:
It was the women who restored us.
I've known them in my time –
mother, sister, teacher, wife,
a green corn row of lovers –
and in my last dry season, going blind,
I look on you who would not yield

to night nor nothing.
I know the end's not chaos,
that you have shaped an end, a destiny
and we shall grow
though we ourselves
ashamed of our own shames
shamed of our need to fight
those last and hardest battles with ourselves,
our waste, our worthlessness
would silence you.

1973-1974

LITTERING EARTH'S CENTRE

"A people scattered and peeled...
a people terrible from their beginning hitherto...
a nation meted out and trodden underfoot..."

Isaiah

I

Manley and Marryshow are dead
and Busta's aged and gaunt,
Butler decrepit.
Our time's a bleeding foetus
spawned of theirs, spawned of the slaves'
seasons of being and begetting –
season on season until Christ knows when.
What turmoil do we leave inheritors?
What wrath, what miseries?

II

But would you say all runs to ruin?
It whirls in chaos, yes,
but is that ruin
or the eternal bongo dance of life and death?
Graves are men's pedestals;
I flute my faith through my ancestral bones
that give my song its meaning and its mirth.
How under God do dead bones live,
in what dread valleys, sepulchres or soils,
except through life they seeded from their loins.

III

Old fiddles rot in corners,
old drums crumble
and their music dies;
ah, but the dancers,
ah, their feet are gay,
the dancers raging
in the generation.

IV

History is a people's compost heap;
midden upon midden upon midden
white's heaped on black on islands,
black on white
and Asia dumped upon our whip-scarred back
keeps sugar roller rolling
in endless treadmill of hard indigence
that says our islands are random dunghills
of slums and barrackyards and gruesome hovels.

V

Bawl murder and let loose the starveling dogs.
Bang every Jesus bell on every steeple.
Come Nazarene at high noon
and cut some cane;
load up a cart or two,
sweat like a slave,
then turn again my master, turn again,
make miracles to remake the folk condition,
ascend Blue Mountains, Soufriere, Tucuche,
preach your sweet sermons there

lest history's and our present weight of wrath
drown you in our long Atlantic swells,
down down beyond all rising and redemption.

VI

Bogle and Gordon.
Gordon and Bogle.
Cry them Caribbean!
Cry all wronged men!
Cry them all martyrdom!
A madman hanged them,
a lunatic in the queen's pay,
a barbarous fanatic wretch
daydreaming blood of niggers
hanged and dangling on his gibbets.
Sweet Christ, are they with Thee in Paradise?

VII

Once Busta worked a Kingston
mob combustible, and Butler,
shouldering Cipriani out,
lit fires in oil and canes
to give their sad slave labour today's meaning.
Moved men make miracles,
the rest churn lies
and history fells them like dead forest trees
and rots their sodden memories like leaves.

VIII

We lurch and rumble,
inching generations on
in cow cart, donkey cart, mule cart
mountained with cane,
each wheel teetering to break its axle
and make mad anarchy in each plantation.
Blood's in our eye this season.
Our sweat turned blood,
drops from those wounds
the thorns, the spear incised,
drips in our hovels of cow dung and marl
and wattles, plyboard, boxboard, cardboard,
discarded flattened drums and cans –
our verminous tenements where hopes sprout
mushrooms poisoning their own marrow, and whores,
pimps, rapists, beggars, thieves, the sordid
populations, swarm and fester.

IX

Gehenna's here and now. Our youth,
wrenched fanatic,
are slain upon our triple ranges.
One scoundrel, hollow as a nutmeg shell,
shreds out his parish on a nutmeg grater
among those other lumps of bull's excreta
steaming in the sun, more names than places,
their indigence more real than their inhabitants,
more harsh than the outcropping of their rock.

X

Ah brother, what's to do?
Acres of shanty town in Port of Spain,
dungle in Kingston town
beyond the boundary of hope,
outside the furthest reaches of our love,
flyblown as offal rotting in the sun
while the rich bore their souls with orgies
and power hoards guns, grenades,
bull pistles and tear gas against its doom.
Gord brudder, what to do?
Jeesas! Gord brudder!
Wha' de arse to do?

XI

Dem communist say "War!"
Dem fat head buaye, dem turn
gorilla eena bush.
Don' even mention dem so.
Baddam! Buddow!
All man fall dead
like deer and quenk and lappe.
Me Baptist leader man
say, "Tek it cool,
walk sorfly, bredren,
talk asy, tek you' time,
onlay say you can' mash ants,
wear blinkers like dem tourist,
close you eye,
tings looking bleak
for nigger people now.
De sign and dem ent good,
de time ent right,

is a nex' slavery days
come back again.
Leh we praise Gord nuh den.
A tekking hymn No. 468
'Peace Perfect Peace…
Our future all unknown…' "

XII

My Jesus thorn tree blooms
blessing the neighbourhood.
Cool water trickles from that Moses rock.
Slender as bamboo shoots
my barefoot girls
cast shadows on my street.
Slums are playing pan
and drumming sweet reggae
transcending wrath
to make all dance
among the ruins of the generation.

XIII

To make all dance,
make mas' and bacchanal in town.
Ah Port of Spain,
assembling your harlequinade
of calypsos, steelbands and masquerade
although guts bleed
and bloated children moan
and beggars blot the pavements
and half the city youth
crowd on its corners dreaming fantasies
of violent hope born of their need,

born of those shabby films of fists and guns
and crazed brutality.
Ah, mine's a town to make all poems mad.

XIV

But art's a state of mind,
a contemplation of the earth and sky,
of man in all conditions and all moods
and of God's cold careless, cold
contemptuous gaze,
his stone-cold unconcern for Adam's heirs.

Where is salvation now?
Where faith and love?
One Jesus had his dream, but we've outgrown it;
one Karl Marx had another but they fouled it
with massacres and mad intransigence.
What phoenix rises now?
All Father, what comes after?
This age is the mad matrix of what age?
All's drowned in blood.
all beauty raped and scarred
and left in sewers
and in the ashes of dead fires.

XV

And still I ask and ask again,
who sends the mad, the lonely and the damned?
Who sent sweet-hearted Amos
and brave Isaiah rapping to their times?
Who sends sculptors, painters, singers, dancers?
Ask Brathwaite who sent him.

Ask him to write that poem of himself
streaming through the loins of slave on slave
century on century
to this outpouring of his crafted verse.
And Walcott too,
he talks like a wise man,
disdainful, cool, offhand, ironical.
And ask that cold, sardonic man
making the perfect fiction,
wrinkling his Brahman nose at islands.
What are they doing on these shattered shores,
droppings of continents,
landscapes of Lilliput,
littering earth's centre,
this Atlantic Ocean?

AT QUINAM BAY

Soparee Mai is still maintained
in her south town of quiet ways
and modest means; and south from there
beyond Mendez, in a green plain
of old oil wells and planted teak,
it is land's end in Quinam Bay.
The road's a black canal to sea
where Colon's schooners rolled off shore
and his boats were lugged to land
cleaving the indifferent wave.
Columbus, weary of the sea,
of tossing an eternity
on Atlantic's murderous wastes,
was sick in flesh and sick at heart
to plunder heathen golden kingdoms
of a glittering continent.
But after wastes of hellish seas
God rewarded him with islands.

Slavers from the Guinea Coast
beyond horizon, stumbled reeking
to this bay, disgorging cargoes
of sick slaves who knew not where
on earth they stood or may be hell.
Had they crossed the Acheron?
The slavers' crews were sick to soul
with shipping men like beasts in chains,
bound beneath decks – grievous voyages
fouling breath and fouling spirit;
a stink, a moaning marred their dreams.
Years afterward they could not eat
for smelling filth and hearing groans;
nor love a woman in a bed
for memories of riven folk

manacled at hand and foot
to the beams on which they lay
wallowing in their nauseous dung.
The very ocean vomited
as each slaver clove her way
from Guinea to the Caribbees.

He's seen and known and done too much;
bone-weary as Colon himself,
soul-wretched as the slavers' crews,
heartsick as any dying slave
he walks to bay,
every dream he dreamed long drowned,
every love sunk underground,
every vision vanished.
Will the sea yield him quiet death.
Wake him a ghost of the despairs
of all the dead who trafficked here?

FINIS

night casts its blanket
on the wood
blacker than blindness

nothing breaks midnight now
the fireflies died
life's candles flickered out

darkness has entered
at the pores of love
and joy and grief
and art and song

now sound is silence
silence
silence

a man has passed
into the heart of darkness

c.1974

APPENDIX OF VARIANT POEMS

ANACAONA

They wrote their names,
Their race, their pride,
Their dancing figures,
All their history
Upon flats of stone
Kept clean in wind and sunlight.
They added daily
To their aging record.

But iron paladins
Ravening from the east
Alighted from the sea like gods
And shouted death.

They shattered the stone records
And they scattered household goods
And gods and blood
Across the hearths and fields.

In the queen's chamber
Earth brown vases
Held the queen's red roses;
Loveliest for the loveliest,
All the best in Xaragua
For Anacaona.
But voices in the courtyard
Cracked like whips,
Like snapping steel.
Mail clanged and jangled
And arms clashed.
The voices cried "Ho!"
The courtiers screamed
"Woe! woe are we!
Woe is Xaragua!

Woe is our queen
Anacoana!"

A sword blade struck
And shattered
All the vases of the roses.
The petals were spattered
Like blood drops
On the draperies.
Gauntletted fingers like talons
Seized the black hair
Of the waiting woman.
The stiff dagger struck.
The queen screamed.
But the don laughed
The snarling laughter
Of the blood chapped lion
Of the hills of Aragon.
He dragged her fainted
Through the palace doors.

In San Domingo plaza
They hung her grimly
On a cold and drizzly dawn.

Trinidad Guardian 1949

THE OLD HOUSE

Here is overgrown desolation of long neglected lawns
About a desolate, broken, wind-moaning house
That grieves in the sun's mirror,
And in the compassionate moon's
Mourns her shattered past-wandered grace.

Remembering her treasures, she remembers a man
Mellow and ripe, sweet as his fruits,
Who raised his seed here;
But the man is dead; and such as he return no more;
With him a species ended;
And his gray widow nods in town among a rude generation.

From clear bells of hearts laughter pealed in the house;
And love was a zephyr, tender and tender,
A mother softly her cradle song crooning.
I knew it, for I, a boy, a stranger walked through their doors,
Found the house gracious and lovely,
Found them brown, rose-mouthed and comely,
Dark-haired and curly, and was joyous among them.
Here with beautiful innocence we laughed our green laughter
Buoyant as birdsong in the woods of our youth.

Wrecked now and crumbled in the corner
Lies the piano that sang us tunes: a very tomb of tunes.
And I remember, Michael,
I remember her whose fingers flitted, tinkling tunes,
Brown fingers lovelier than tunes
Now white and fleshless skeleton;
And I must lie upon the broken floor
And weep into the urn of the dead years.

And weep for her the wounded swan caged in grim rooms,
Dreaming deceiving images of days beyond gray walls;
All her people the passers, strangers to and fro,
The sick, the dying, the touring doctors:
Oh, I mourn her death, her endless resurrection of dawns
To the tomb of her hopes.

And for the last, the widowed one,
Measuring miserly days in town,
Measuring her drams of tears for the lover
Cheated away into the lap of the clay,
Measuring the growth of her children against the post of the years
Measuring the failing light of her beauty,
I weep and I weep,

But, for you and I, Michael,
The careless, cloud-laurelled jongleurs of life,
We whom the sun refills,
And the moon of her mercy gives new wine for our wounds
When the tigress thing at our hearts
And the jealous world would bind us and blind us and strike us dumb –
What are tears? What are tears?

Here in your ruinous house, my Jonathan, where we were young,
I write upon the stained and broken panes the canzones of our blood,
The lilting rhythms of our lyric hearts.
And the black bird of death, the king corbeau upon my shoulder perched.
He scratches out the words mingling the indifferent dust.
The song floats formless in the silent air
Among the ghosts of songs anonymous:
I laugh, re-echoing your laughter were you here.

Bim, 1951

HOMESTEAD

Seven cedars break the Trades
From the thin gables of my house:
I know the green demonic rage
When gales are trapped in their thick foliage
But weathers turn, the drought returns,
The great sun burns the green to ochre
Dry racking winds knock the boughs bare
Till they are tragic stands of sticks
Pitiful in pitiless noons
But know dusk's bounty and the moon's.

Beyond the cedars there are fields
Where one man sweated out his days
Wearying his stubborn bone.
He'd bought thick woodland for his own,
Set his axe of hope upon it
With his rugged bones of courage
And left his sons an heritage.
This heavy drudgery for a man
But plants his spirit in the earth
That blooms no fragrance of his worth.

So I write his epitaph
In his own blood of hope and faith:
"His life was simple peasant bread,
"He wrote his memoirs in his head,
"His heavy labour drained his face,
"He felt to his arthritic bone
"Both our weathers of the sun.
"God was his good friend on his fields
"In changing skies and wind and rain;
"He harvested his faith in grain".

Though his heavy days are done
He is present in the fields
In natural holy images.
He's girth and growth of all his trees,
He's on these tracks his goings made
In his slow to and fro in boots
As Earthy as his nurtured roots
To every furrow of the land.
To every shaken grace of grass
He is the spirit of the place.

An unnamed, unknown slaveman's son;
Paysan, paisano; of all common
Men time-long in fields world over
In the cotton, corn and clover
Who are not told, but tell their breed
Through history's book, as passive, as
Unkillable as common grass;
Whose temperate and patient soul
The heavy loam of human earth
Feeds woods of wisdom, art and faith.

Kyk-over-Al, 1957

HOMESTEAD

Seven splendid cedars break the trades
From the thin gables of my house,
Seven towers of song when the trades rage
Through their full green season foliage.
But weathers veer, the drought returns,
The sun burns emerald to ochre
And thirsty winds strip the boughs bare,
Then they are tragic stands of sticks
Pitiful in pitiless noons
And wear dusk's buskin and the moon's.

And north beyond them lie the fields
Which one man laboured his life's days,
One man wearying his bone
Shaped them as monuments in stone,
Hammered them with iron will
And a rugged earthy courage,
And going, left me heritage.
Is labour lovely for a man
That drags him daily into earth
Returns no fragrance of him forth?

The man is dead but I recall
Him in my voluntary verse,
His life was unadorned as bread,
He reckoned weathers in his head
And wore their ages on his face
And felt their keenness to his bone
The sting of sun and whip of rain.
He read day's event from the dawn
And saw the quality of morning
Through the sunset mask of evening.

In the fervour of my song
I hold him firm upon the fields
In many homely images.
His ghost's as tall as the tall trees;
He tramps these tracks his business made
By daily roundabout in boots
Tougher and earthier than roots;
And every furrow of the earth
And every shaken grace of grass
Knows him the spirit of the place.

He was a slave's son, peasant born,
Paisan, paisano – those common
Men about their fields, world over,
Of sugar, cotton, corn or clover
Who are unsung but who remain
Perpetual as the passing wind,
Unkillable as the frail grass;
Who, from their graves within their graves,
Nourish the splendour of the earth
And give her substance, give her worth.

Poets and artists turn again,
Construct your cunning tapestries
Upon the ages of their acres,
The endless labours of their years;
Still at the centre of their world
Cultivate the first green graces,
Courage, strength and kindliness,
Love of man and beast and landscape;
Still sow and graft the primal good,
Green boughs of innocence to God.

The Sun's Eye, 1968

POEM

Pray that the poem come out of the dark
Like clear spring water jetting from a rock,
Like blossom crowning the green blossomer,
And go with the white pride of cumuli,
And sing like light dawn's silver villanelle;
Pray for the phrases of the wheeling Trades.

Praise out of heart her whole and hybrid beauty
Now that her bone stands up among upstanding
Beauty of boughs blossoming flame and flames
Leaping and falling in fields, on hearths, in hearts
Tender and kind in their first uttering love;
Praise her great rose among the season's roses.

A viking roving from his temperate island
Greeted our islands where the intemperate sun
Hurled darts of torrid light against his eyes,
Kindled wild torrid passion in his heart
For dark desire whirling through her drums:
She is their seed, the passion and the dark.

She's not what you have seen – that Doric stone,
Those flanks and breasts amazing gods and men;
That form was cut for a coarse artisan
Who was half blind from soot in his black forge –
She is the dancer in dreams, the grace in the tides,
The flower of foam that gleamed at Paphos, goddess,
Goddess, eternally woman, legend and living.
Lancelot and Tristan drank a dolorous wine
From golden beakers through audacious days.
Abelard prayed his sin round a swan's neck.
And Goya's duchess blazed, and Rembrandt's wife;
And each new poet speaks new sonnets to her.

Kyk-over-Al, No 22, 1957

A REED FOR MY RIME

(For Maeve Elliot)

Lodged over and against the sea you hear
Continually her grief and rage;
Continually your heart is chasmed to her passage
And her pouring through the arteries of your being,
The bay of your dwelling.

Oh, she is in us green as spring,
As growing in a season's raining,
As life's beginnings, evergreen.
We were firstborn of her, not beautifully
Though as Botticelli dreamed of Aphrodite
In soft goddess grace, in flowering glory.

The blood is sea-taste still,
And lymph is pale as the sea's submarine streams
And colourless oozing sap of the sea's bones.
We are her foundlings; the nomad moon
Sways the blood's tides, currents of desire
Drag and foam and fret in the generant flesh,
And the single, secret, seaborn amoeba begins generation.

The sea is the folktale of our grief:
We groaned in her green jaws in a crazed time,
In the Trades' strength, in the tiger's yawn,
Of the torrid doldrum; we had not dreamed such water
Who had only known rivers and torrents
And the mammoth land rolling and mountainous.
But by the earth's grace we crawled out upon the islands
To leech again like trilobite to rock.

Oh, our gods fled from us, and our speech
Fell down precipitous silence,
And the seeds of our blood were wasted as tares.
History is a bewildering nightmare,
Bitter herbs to eat, vinegar and myrrh,
Anger and anguish to wear through our days.
What faiths shall we feel,
What rose bloom from the trodden stone of our heart?

I fly the scene of my resentment
To wander alien, footloose, rootless,
A Jew, a gipsy on the seabeat rock;
But yet I swarm with a fierce love for us
the continentals broken up on islands;
An acute hurting love like a disease,
A green parochial aching in the heart.
I am wrecked on the soul's shores,
Washed by our tragic memory of tears
Till in my singing, heart, hand, harp
Are grief with the willow's grief,
With the river's continuity of sorrow.

Beauty walks rarely in the midst of all;
The lily sparks the drought, the rock-growth flowers
Clusters white as cumulus; you walk in the sun,
A dark moon-goddess ravishing the day,
And hates and fears are fathoms drowned
Beneath your wave you lovely of the land.
We had been taller once and danced,
But never lovelier than since to Cancer's mood
The Trades sway free and Aphrodite's voice
Is soft with rising laughter like the wind.

BBC *Caribbean Voices*, Script Number 923, March 14, 1954

city centre '70

here at the city centre,
in this sweet square
the stone men closed,
the trees green witness
that men do not die
but grow in dreams of generations
bitter and beautiful as cedar leaves,
by flooding tides of wrath and beauty
in the harsh comedy of history,
that love distils like mountain springs
from the diseased blood of tyranny
and shame's corruption that shut up the square.

in their green immortality
the trees condescend that we,
wayfarers in the traffic
and in time, should see
them with unseeing eyes
blind to their beauty
coolly statued in eternity
here where we've jailed them
in the square, forlorn
as exile on the Boca rock.

their laurels crown
their great immobile marathons:
applauses, flowers, flames
well up in silent seasonal surges,
green fails to brown
and brownness, the earth's colour,
sinks to earth where the sweet
cycle reaffirms itself,
rejoins eternity and greens again
in the triumphant self-regenerating trees.

SAG., Vol. 1, No. 3, Dec. 1970, p. 52.

INDEX OF FIRST LINES

SOURCES OF PUBLISHED POEMS

(A chronology of publications, re-publications, and broadcasts)

1. "New Year",[1] *The Teachers' Herald*, Vol. 5 no. 53 (Jan. 1938) p. 2.
2. "A Night of Stars", *The Teachers' Herald*, Vol. 5 no. 53 (Jan. 1938) p. 38.
3. "Immortelles" (The forest flames),[1] *The Teachers' Herald*, Vol. 5 no. 54 (Feb. 1938) pp. 28-29.
4. "Immortelles" (Earth decks herself),[1] *The Teachers' Herald*, Vol. 5 no. 55 (Mar. 1938) p. 28.
5. "Discovery",[1] *The Teachers' Herald*, Vol. 6 no. 60 (Aug. 1938) pp. 21-22.
6. "Death on Sunday",[1] *The Teachers' Herald*, Vol. 6 no. 61 (Sept. 1938) pp. 29.
7. "A Poet Passes",[1] *The Teachers' Herald*, Vol. 6 no. 63 (Nov. 1938) p. 31.
8. "The Tragedy",[1] *The Teachers' Herald*, Vol. 6 no. 64 (Dec. 1938) p. 31.
9. "To Learie", *Trinidad Guardian*, Jan. 19, 1939, p. 13.
10. "The Stair of Song", *Sunday Guardian*, Jan. 29, 1939, p. 30.
11. "Folly", *Trinidad Guardian*, Feb. 16, 1939, p. 13.
12. "Tonight, Tomorrow",[2] *Sunday Guardian*, July 23, 1939, p. 20.
13. "New Loaves",[1] *Best Poems of Trinidad*, p. 31.
14. "Death on Sunday",[1] *Best Poems of Trinidad*, p. 32.
15. "Song of the Sleepers-Out", *Trinidad Guardian*, Sept. 19, 1944, p. 4.
16. "Tribute to Winifred Atwell", *Sunday Guardian*, Oct. 1, 1944, p. 4.
17. "For Freedom", *Trinidad Guardian*, Dec. 5, 1944, p. 4.
18. "Carib and Arawak",[1] *The Teachers' Herald*, Vol. 9 no. 139/140 (Aug./Sep. 1945).
19. "Colour (for Harold Telemaque)", *Guardian Weekly Magazine*, Jan. 5, 1947, p. 8.
20. "Hurricane Hill", *Guardian Weekly Magazine*, Aug. 8, 1948, p. 10.

21. "A Lover Speaks", *Guardian Weekly Magazine*, Oct. 10, 1948, p. 10.

22. "Sounds Live", *Guardian Weekly Magazine*, Nov. 14, 1948, p. 10.

23. "Dusk", *Guardian Weekly Magazine*, Dec. 12, 1948, p. 10.

24. "She (for Basil Pitt)", *Guardian Weekly Magazine*, Feb. 6, 1949, p. 14.

25. "*Anacaona*", *Guardian Weekly Magazine*, Feb. 27, 1949, p. 10.

26. "Invocation", *Caribbean Voices*, London: BBC, Aug. 21, 1949.

27. "March Trades", *Caribbean Voices*, London: BBC, Aug. 21, 1949.

28. "Shallow Underground", *Caribbean Voices*, London: BBC, Aug. 21, 1949.

29. "Token", *Caribbean Voices*, London: BBC, Aug. 21, 1949.

30. "The Old Man", *Caribbean Voices*, London: BBC, Aug. 21, 1949.

31. "Poem" (June blazes), *TGW*, Oct. 9, 1949, p. 4.

32. "Oh, No More Now", *TGW*, Dec. 18, 1949, p. 4.

33. "Oh, No More Now", *Bim* 11 (Dec. 1949), p. 240.

34. "Stranger, Beware", *Bim* 11 (Dec. 1949), p. 247.

35. "February", *Caribbean Voices*, London: BBC, May 21, 1950.

36. "The Flowering Rock", *Caribbean Voices*, London: BBC, May 21, 1950.

37. "Oh, No More Now", *Caribbean Voices*, London: BBC, May 21, 1950.

38. "The Flowering Rock", *Bim* 12 (June 1950), p. 274.

39. "Beyond", *Bim* 12 (June 1950), p. 275.

40. "Death Does Not", *Bim* 12 (June 1950), p. 275-6.

41. "Frigate Bird Passing", *Bim* 13 (June 1950), p. 36.

42. "Transition", *Bim* 13 (June 1950), p. 37.

43. "Poets and Painters", *Caribbean Voices*, London: BBC, Aug. 20, 1950.

44. "Dancer", *Guardian Weekly Magazine*, Nov. 26, 1950, p. 10.

45. "Poem (He plucked a burning stylus)", *Guardian Weekly Magazine*, Nov. 26, 1950, p. 10.

46. "Eclogue for Christmas", *Sunday Guardian*, Dec. 24, 1950, p. 6.

47. "Poem (He Plucked a Burning Stylus)", *Bim* 14 (June 1951), p. 106.

48. "Birth (for Judith Herbert)", *Bim* 15 (June 1951), p. 181.

49. "The Old House", *Bim* 15 (June 1951), pp. 181-2.

50. "Letter to Lamming in England", *Caribbean Voices*, London: BBC, Apr. 13, 1952.

51. "Homestead", *Caribbean Voices*, London: BBC, Apr. 13, 1952.

52. "Men", *Caribbean Voices*, London: BBC, Apr. 13, 1952.

53. "Stranger, Beware", *Kyk-over-al* 4:4 (June 1952), p. 47.

54. "The Flowering Rock", *Kyk-over-al* 4:4 (June 1952), p. 48.

55. "Poem (He Plucked a Burning Stylus)", *Kyk-over-al* 4:4 (June 1952), p. 49.

56. "Tree." *Bim* 16 (June 1952), pp. 261-2.

57. "Something Seen", *Bim* 16 (June 1952), pp. 262-3.

58. "Letter to Lamming in England", *Bim* 17 (Dec. 1952) pp. 36-37.

59. "Homestead", *Caribbean Quarterly* 2:3 (1952), pp. 54-5.

60. "Black Gods", *Caribbean Voices*, London: BBC, Feb. 22, 1953.

61. "Black Kings", *Caribbean Voices*, London: BBC, Feb. 22, 1953.

62. "A Tear for Toussaint", *Caribbean Voices*, London: BBC, Feb. 22, 1953.

63. "Despite Ancestral Rape", *Caribbean Voices*, London: BBC, Mar. 8, 1953.

64. "I Walk Abroad", *Caribbean Voices*, London: BBC, Mar. 8, 1953.

65. "New Year Poem for Cecil Herbert", *Caribbean Voices*, London: BBC, Mar. 8, 1953.

66. "Caribbean Coronation Verse", *Caribbean Voices*, London: BBC, May 31, 1953.

67. "Caribbean Coronation Verse", *Bim* 18 (June 1953), pp. 82-3.

68. "In Mango Shade", *Caribbean Voices*, London: BBC, Aug. 16, 1953.

69. "Legend of Daaga", *Caribbean Voices*, London: BBC, Nov. 22, 1953.

70. "Poem (Pray That the Poem Out of Nowhere Come)", *Bim* 19 (Dec. 1953), p. 179.

71. "The Fighters", *Bim* 19 (Dec. 1953), pp. 227-8.

72. "A Dirge for a Dead Poet", *Caribbean Voices*, London: BBC, Mar. 14, 1954

73. "Cradlesong, for Judith", *Caribbean Voices*, London: BBC, Mar. 14, 1954.

74. "A Reed for My Rime (for Maeve Elliot)", *Caribbean Voices*, London: BBC, Mar. 14, 1954.

75. "The White Coffin (for Jean Herbert)", *Bim* 20 (June 1954), p. 290.

76. "A Dirge for a Dead Poet", *Bim* 20 (June 1954), p. 303.

77. "Lady by the Sea (for Maeve Elliott)", *Bim* 21 (Dec. 1954), pp. 14-15.

78. "At Grafton Bay", *Bim* 21 (Dec. 1954), p. 15.

79. "Troy World", *Bim* 22 (June 1955), p. 72.

80. "Hawk Heart", *Bim* 22 (June 1955), p. 119.

81. "The Legend of Anacaona", *Caribbean Voices*, London: BBC, Aug. 14, 1955.

82. "Ballad of Canga", *Caribbean Voices*, London: BBC, Aug. 14, 1955.

83. "The Old House", *Caribbean Voices*, London: BBC, Aug. 14, 1955.

84. "For the Peasant People of the Islands", *Caribbean Voices*, London: BBC, Aug. 14, 1955.

85. "Corn", *Caribbean Voices*, London: BBC, Aug. 14, 1955.

86. "To My Mother", *Caribbean Voices*, London: BBC, Oct. 9, 1955.

87. "The Blind Weavers", *Caribbean Voices*, London: BBC, Oct. 9, 1955.

88. "Doggerel for Adolescence", *Bim* 23 (Dec. 1955), p. 182.

89. "Ballad of Canga", *Caribbean Quarterly* 4:2 (1955), pp. 165-6.

90. "Love Overgrows a Rock", *Bim* 25 (July-Dec. 1957), p. 16.

91. "Homestead", *Kyk-over-al* 22 (1957), pp. 52-53.

92. "To My Mother", *Kyk-over-al* 22 (1957), pp. 53-54.

93. "Poem (Pray that the Poem Come Out of the Dark)", *Kyk-over-al* 22 (1957), pp. 54-55.

94. "Poem (He Plucked a Burning Stylus)", *Kyk-over-al* 22 (1957), p. 55.

95. "I am the Archipelago", *Kyk-over-al* 22 (1957), p. 56.

96. "Fugue for Federation", *Bim* 26 (Jan.-June 1958), pp. 75-76.

97. "To My Mother", *Caribbean Quarterly* 5:3 (1958), p. 180.

98. "Lady by the Sea", *Caribbean Quarterly* 5:3 (1958), p. 181.

99. "Homestead", *Caribbean Quarterly* 5:3 (1958), p. 183.

100. "Homestead", *Caribbean Voices*, London: BBC, July 13, 1958. This is a rebroadcast of 1952 programme.

101. "Corn", *Kyk-over-al* 24 (Dec. 1958), p. 47.

102. "The Blind Weavers", *Kyk-over-al* 24 (Dec. 1958), p. 48.

103. "She Never Dies", *Bim* 28 (Jan.-June 1959), p. 198.

104. "For A. A. Cipriani", *Bim* 29 (July-Dec. 1959), p. 41.

105. "Notes for a New Poem", *Opus: A Review* (June, 1960), p. 10.

106. "The Picture", *Bim* 31 (July-Dec. 1960), p. 148.

107. "Homestead", *Tamarack Review* 14 (Winter, 1960), pp. 74-75.

108. "The Old Woman", *Kyk-over-al* 27 (Dec. 1960), p. 72.

109. "He Juggles Images", *Bim* 32 (Jan.-June 1961), pp. 251-2.

110. "The Curse of Her Beauty", *Bim* 32 (Jan.-June 1961), pp. 252-253.

111. "Mother and Son", *Bim* 33 (July-Dec. 1961), p. 7.

112. "The World of Islands", *Bim* 34 (Jan.-June 1962), p. 81.

113. "I am the Archipelago", *Sunday Guardian* Nov. 29, 1964, p. 21.

114. "I am the Archipelago", *London Magazine* Vol. 5, no. 6 (Sept. 1965) p. 23.

115. "Ballad of Canga", *London Magazine* Vol. 5, no. 6 (Sept. 1965), pp. 24-26

116. "Caribbean Calypso", *Verse and Voice* (1965), pp. 71-73. This is a revision of "Caribbean Coronation Verse".

117. "Homestead", *Young Commonwealth Poets '65*, p. 205.

118. "The Picture", *Caribbean Literature* (1966), p. 56.

119. "February", *Caribbean Voices* (John Figueroa, 1966), v. 1, pp. 21-22.

120. "Ballad of Canga", *Caribbean Verse* (1967), pp. 57-59.

121. "To My Mother." *Caribbean Verse*, pp. 59-61.

122. "Poets and Painters," *A Collection of Poems* (1967), p. 1.

123. "Caribbean Calypso", *A Collection of Poems*, p. 2.

124. "Love Overgrows a Rock", *A Collection of Poems*, p. 5.

125. "February", *A Collection of Poems*, p. 6.

126. "The Picture", *New Voices of the Commonwealth* (1968), pp. 81-82.

127. "The World of Islands", *New Voices of the Commonwealth* (1968), p. 82.

128. "I am the Archipelago", *New Voices of the Commonwealth* (1968), p. 83.

129. "Homestead." *The Sun's Eye* (1968), p. 116.

130. "At Guaracara Park", *Studio Arts Group* 1:3 (Dec. 1970), p. 17.

131. "City Centre '70", *Studio Arts Group* 1:3 (Dec. 1970), p. 41.

132. "March Trades," *Caribbean Voices*, (Figueroa, 1970) v. 2, pp. 155-56.

133. "Caribbean Calypso", *Caribbean Voices*, (Figueroa, 1970) v. 2, pp. 178-181.

134. "Love Overgrows a Rock", *Caribbean Voices*, (Figueroa, 1970) v. 2, p. 216.

135. "Poem (Dying, the Serpent's…)", *Tapia* 1:25 (April 2, 1972), p. 2.

136. "Poem for this Day", *Tapia* 2:11 (Dec. 17, 1972), p. 14.

137. "City Centre '70", *New Writing in the Caribbean* (1972), pp. 88-89. This is an enlarged version.

138. "Ballad for Tubal Butler", *New Writing in the Caribbean* (1972), p. 88.

139. "Elegy for N. Manley", *New Writing in the Caribbean* (1972), pp. 89-90.

140. "Piarco", *New Writing in the Caribbean* (1972), pp. 91-92.

141. "Blues for Uncle Tom", *The Black I* 1:1 (March, 1972), p. 54. The name of journal often given incorrectly. Williams gives 1972; Gianetti gives 1970. My text is from typescript Selected poems at St. Augustine.

142. "Hard Drought", *Tapia* 3:16 (April 22, 1973), p. 5.

143. "Letter to Lamming in England", *Savacou* 7/8 (1973), pp. 66-67.

144. "Verse in August", *Savacou* 7/8 (1973), pp. 97-100.

145. "I am the Archipelago", *You Better Believe It* (1973), pp. 156-158.

146. "Homestead", *Breaklight* (1973), pp. 98-100.

147. "Love Overgrows a Rock", *Caribbean Rhythms* (1974), pp. 177-178.

148. "March Trades", *Caribbean Rhythms* (1974), 178-179.
149. "Ballad of Canga", *The Caribbean Poem* (1976), pp. 88-89.
150. "Verse in August", *The Caribbean Poem* (1976), pp. 90-92.
151. "City Centre '70", *Nine West Indian Poets* (1980), p. 56.
152. "Piarco", *Nine West Indian Poets* (1980), pp. 57-58.
153. "Homestead", *Nine West Indian Poets* (1980), pp. 59-60.
154. "Elegy for N. Manley", *Nine West Indian Poets* (1980), pp. 61-62.
155. "To My Mother", *Nine West Indian Poets* (1980), 62-63.
156. "To My Mother", *Caribbean Poetry Now* (1984), p. 11.
     1984
157. "Love Overgrows a Rock", *The Penguin Book of Caribbean Verse* (1986), p.173.
158. "Piarco", *The Penguin Book of Caribbean Verse* (1986), pp. 174-75.
159. "At Guaracara Park", *The Penguin Book of Caribbean Verse* (1986), pp. 175-76.
160. "Hard Drought", *Voiceprint* (1989), pp. 74-75.
161. "Verse in August", *Voiceprint* (1989), pp. 75-78.
162. "I am the Archipelago", *Voiceprint* (1989), 196-197.
163. "Transition", *Voiceprint* (1989), pp. 265-266.

compiled by L. A. Breiner, 1985-91, 2012.

1. – by "Merton Maloney"
2. – by "Merton Roach"

References for Anthologies:

Best Poems of Trinidad, Ed. A. M. Clarke (Trinidad: Frasers Printerie, 1943).
Young Commonwealth Poets '65, Ed. P. L. Brent (London: Heinemann, 1965).
Caribbean Literature, Ed. G. R. Coulthard (London: Univ. of London Press, 1966).

Caribbean Voices, Ed. John Figueroa. Vol.1 (London: Evans Brothers, 1966).

Caribbean Verse, Ed. O. R. Dathorne (London: Heinemann, 1967).

A Collection of Poems by a Poet of Tobago E. M. Roach, (Tobago: Conference of Heads of Carib. Univs., Apr. 1967).

New Voices of the Commonwealth, Ed. H. Sargeant (London: Evans Brothers, 1968).

The Sun's Eye, Ed. Anne Walmsley (London: Longmans, 1968).

Caribbean Voices, Ed. John Figueroa. Vol. 2 (London: Evans Brothers, 1970).

New Writing in the Caribbean, Ed. A. J. Seymour (Georgetown: Guyana Lithographic, 1972).

You Better Believe It: Black Verse in English, Ed. Paul Breman (Harmondsworth: Penguin, 1973).

Breaklight, Ed. Andrew Salkey (Garden City: Doubleday, 1973).

Caribbean Rhythms, Ed. James T. Livingston (New York: Washington Square Press, 1974).

The Caribbean Poem, Ed. Neville Dawes & Anthony McNeill (Kingston: Quikprinters, 1976).

Nine West Indian Poets, Ed. Velma Pollard (London: Collins, 1980).

Caribbean Poetry Now, Ed. Stewart Brown (London: Hodder and Stoughton, 1984).

The Penguin Book of Caribbean Verse, Ed. Paula Burnett (Harmondsworth: Penguin, 1986).

Voiceprint, Ed. Stewart Brown, Mervyn Morris, Gordon Rohlehr (London: Longman, 1989).

BIOGRAPHICAL NOTE

Eric Merton Roach was born 3rd November 1915 in Mount Pleasant, Tobago. He became a school teacher after leaving Bishop's High School in Tobago. He joined the army in Trinidad in 1939. After the war he returned to Tobago as a civil servant. He married in December 1952 and in 1954 he left his job to devote his time to writing. In 1960 he returned to teaching and moved to Trinidad in 1961, where he worked chiefly as a journalist. In 1973 he again resigned in order to devote more time to his writing.

He committed suicide by swimming out to sea in April 1974.

In addition to the poems collected in this volume, he was the author of an unpublished novel, a radio serial and three plays, *Belle Fanto* (1967), *Letter from Leonora* (1968) and *A Calabash of Blood* (1971), all published by the Extra Mural Department of the University of the West Indies.

His writing has appeared in many anthologies, including: *Sun's Eye, Caribbean Poetry Now, Penguin Book of Caribbean Verse, Voiceprint, Anthology of Caribbean Verses, and Anthology of Caribbean Short Stories*.

He was awarded the Trinidad and Tobago National Humming Bird Gold Medal, posthumously, in August 1974. He refused offers of university scholarships during his teaching, army and civil service careers.

FURTHER READING

Laurence A. Breiner
Black Yeats: Eric Roach and the Politics of Caribbean Poetry
ISBN: 9781845230470; pp. 312; pub. March 2008; price: £16.99

For readers of West Indian literature, a study of Eric Roach requires no justification. He is the most significant poet in the English-speaking Caribbean between Claude McKay (who spent nearly all of his life abroad) and Derek Walcott. Roach began publishing in the late 1930s and continued, with a few interruptions, until 1974, the year of his suicide. His career thus spans an extraordinary period of Anglophone Caribbean history, from the era of violent strikes that led to the formation of most of the region's political parties, through the process of decolonization, the founding and subsequent failure of the Federation of the West Indies (1958-1962), and the coming of Independence in the 1960s. This book presents a critical analysis of all of Roach's published poetry, but it presents that interpretation as part of a broader study of the relations between his poetic activity, the political events he experienced (especially West Indian Federation, Independence, the Black Power movement, the "February Revolution" of 1970 Trinidad), and the seminal debates about art and culture in which he participated.

By exploring Roach's work within its conditions, this book aims above all to confirm Roach's rightful place among West Indian and metropolitan poets of comparable gifts and accomplishments.

Laurence Breiner is the author of the critically acclaimed *Introduction to West Indian Poetry*.